Sales Funnel
for OMG ROI

Barbara Loraine, MA

LEGAL NOTICE

Dedication

You each know why this book is dedicated to you: Joe, Jay, Jackie, Carla, Kendra, Allison, Adam, Ryleigh, Lincoln, Logan, Jack, Jacquie, Anna, and Joy.

Acknowledgments

To my CEO Space International family,
especially Berny and September Dohrmann.
Also to Greg S. Reid, Eric Lofholm, Bob Proctor,
Anthony Robbins, Jeanette Joy Fisher,
Cynthia Hopper, and Drew Berman

Table of Contents

DEDICATION 11

ACKNOWLEDGMENTS..12

PREFACE...15

SECTION 1- ABOUT THE SALES FUNNEL:...16

CHAPTER 2 - WHY YOU NEED A SALES FUNNEL 22

CHAPTER 3 -SALES FUNNEL OVERVIEW:...25

CHAPTER 4 - KNOW YOUR NUMBERS..36

CHAPTER 5 – LEAN LEAD GENERATION 40

CHAPTER 6 – MAKING SALES...45

CHAPTER 7 – SALES FUNNEL, A CLOSER LOOK..49

SECTION 2 - YOUR PRODUCTS: 69

CHAPTER 8 – BUYER PSYCHOLOGY...70

CHAPTER 9 – YOUR MARKET & OPPORTUNITIES 81

CHAPTER 10 – YOUR PRODUCTS...72

CHAPTER 11 - PRODUCE YOUR PRODUCTS 83

CHAPTER 12 - YOUR IRRESISTIBLE LEAD MAGNET..99

CHAPTER 13 - YOUR COMPELLING FRONT END 108

CHAPTER 15 – YOUR CROSS SELL CAN GENERATE *35% MORE SALES 126

CHAPTER 16 - DOWN SELL FOR MORE SALES 129

CHAPTER 17 - YOUR 2ND, 3RD & MORE UP SELLS 134

CHAPTER 18 – BIG-BUCKS BACK ENDS 142

CHAPTER 19 - FOLLOW-UP EMAILS THAT SELL..159

CHAPTER 20 - 85 WAYS TO THRILL WITH YOUR CUSTOMER EXPERIENCE 171

CHAPTER 21 - WHAT IS NEXT?..178

PREFACE

In this book, I will reveal techniques businesspeople use to double or even triple their revenues. By implementing the Sales Funnel in your business, you can get immediate results . . . as in increased sales. Finally, you can stop worrying about how to get more business and take action to build the pieces required to improve your path to success.

The Sales Funnel serves consumers, too. After all, people want solutions to their problems, as well as fulfillment of their emotional (and other) needs. If they don't buy, they stay unfulfilled. And if they don't buy from you, they may end up with inferior solutions, not nearly as good as what they would get with you.

Sales are the engine that drives corporate America . . . and your small business. The quote below is as relevant today as when it was first spoken. Sales are the key ingredient to any business venture.
I am going to lead you through the steps of setting up your own Sales Funnel. A good Sales Funnel is designed to achieve fast results and to increase your revenue.

SECTION 1:

ABOUT THE
SALES FUNNEL

1 The Sales Funnel Blueprint

Marketing has evolved throughout the years. From billboards in the 1800's, to radio in 1920, and TV ads in 1940, to today with viral advertising on computers and on mobile devices everywhere.

Some things have stayed the same. We still must get "Attention, Interest, Desire, and Action" in order to make the sale. (AIDA is attributed to American advertising and sales pioneer, E. St. Elmo Lewis)

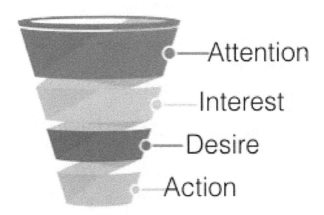

But, when it comes to methods and technologies, to borrow the phrase from an old cigarette ad, "We've come a long way, Baby." Consumers' and buyers' behaviors have changed. The market has changed. Savvy marketers must change, too.

There have been a couple significant changes.

It used to be that Internet businesses offered just one product - not anymore. Through the years, businesses have grown by offering more products. Consumers expect brands to serve many of their needs. Companies selling on the

1) Internet simply had to catch up to that practice. Once you have a market, sell them more of what they want.

2) Salesmen used to go for a close as soon as possible. "Always be closing," was the mantra of those days. Now, consumers like to sample wares upfront, before

3) buying. And "closing" might mean enticing prospects to first consume a free offer to establish trust, providing prospects with an opportunity to first "kick the tires" before making a purchase.

The following image shows the highlights of marketing and advertising changes over time. With technology, changes occur at an accelerated pace and it can be difficult for marketers to keep up.

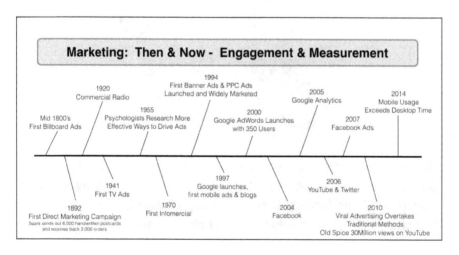

The good news is marketing is more affordable now than ever before. With the Internet, every business person can afford to get in front of their market. But, competition for eyeballs and mindshare is keen. While costs for leads are lower, we must still seek the best possible return on what we invest in lead generation.

Changes happen rapidly. Thanks to the evolution of Internet in the past decades, the national and international reaches of brands have quickly multiplied.

With more and more differences, market segments, and audiences, things have to change. Internet businesses have kept up with the speed of the changes and adapted to – and created – consumer demands.

Now, consumers expect a one-step-at-a-time approach in marketing. In his book, "Jab, Jab, Right Hook," marketing wizard Gary Vaynerchuck spells out how to "give, give and then ask." It's the "Law of Reciprocity" in action. When you first give to people, especially when the gift is of clear value, people feel obligated to buy. Your brand is appreciated and consumers choose you for their purchases.

The Sales Funnel is the marketing system that astute businesspeople use. When it comes to competition, if you are not using a Sales Funnel in your business, you cannot keep up, you are leaving money on the table. Period.

It reminds me of the old story:

Two campers are walking through the woods when a huge brown bear suddenly appears in the clearing about 50 feet in front of them. The bear sees the campers and begins to head toward them. The first guy drops his backpacks, digs out a pair of sneakers, and frantically begins to put them on. The second guy says, "What are you doing? Sneakers won't help you outrun that bear." "I don't need to outrun the bear," the first guy says, "I just need to outrun you."

But, you don't only have to be better (or faster) at what you offer, but you have to be in alignment with consumers' values, emotional needs and desires.

People's desires have expanded – so has the competition to fulfill those wants.
To stay on Apple as an example, Simon Sinek, in his most-watched TedTalk, tells how Apple leads the market. People buy Apple because the brand stands for values and characteristics that people aspire and relate to. With the right message, people want to be like you, they like you, and they buy from you. People buy the "why" behind the brand, especially when it matches their own values and self-image.

We used to say, "Build it and they will come." Now, it's, "You've got an audience, what more do they want to buy from you?" How can you serve them more? And how can you give your customers a better experience along the way?"

Consumers want convenient shopping. They don't want to search high and low for the best providers. They want you to provide them with the proof and the follow through. Further, once they have heard about you, they don't want to remember who you are. They want they want you to be there, easily accessible, when they are ready to buy.

One of life's fundamental truths states,

'Ask and you shall receive.' As kids we get

used to asking for things, but somehow we

lose this ability in adulthood. We come up with

all sorts of excuses and reasons to avoid

any possibility of criticism or rejection.

- Jack Canfield

Chapter 2 - Why You Need a Sales Funnel

We all want to maximize profits from the leads we pay for, don't we?

As mentioned earlier, Internet marketing has changed from selling only one product to the Sales Funnel model. Why? Because offering only one product produces low return on investment, we leave money on the table.

But, it's also about serving your prospects and clients. Prospects want to learn more about you and to feel more confident that you will deliver value, before making a big financial commitment.

With internet marketing, the Sales Funnel makes it easier for people to buy with: a free sample (**Lead Magnet**), then a small purchase (**Front End**), so they can gain confidence while experiencing how the provider delivers results. As the Sales Funnel progresses, each product offers more and more value than the one before, often at higher and higher prices (**Up Sell #1, #2, and more**). There are also add-on products (**Cross Sell**), and the high-end and recurring payment (**Back End**) products. Later, we'll give complete descriptions of these products, along with examples and when an how to use which kind of product.

The Sales Funnel - Products

Lead Magnet	Front End	UpSell #1	Cross Sell
Down Sell	UpSell #2	UpSell #3	Back End

In the past, Internet marketers used to sell only one product and they still made money. Internet marketing giant, Frank Kern, started out with one product, how teach a bird to sing. As we've said, to maximize your ROI from the leads you get and your list, better to have a Sales Funnel with several product offerings.

However, there are exceptions. An example is Neil Patel. He offers free big-value webinars, and then goes straight for the $1,000 product purchase. But, there's a reason why he's an exception. He's been around the Internet marketing world for years, he's famous in the industry, and he has a proven track record. Want to know more about him? There's lots of social proof of his expertise. Plus, in his case, he has other streams of income from his other businesses and products. He's founder of Crazy Egg, KISSmetrics, and Hello Bar. He doesn't need to maximize profits from his training program. His clients include top brands who pay very big bucks.

I still work hard to know my business.

I'm continuously looking for ways

to improve all my companies,

and I'm always selling. Always.

- Mark Cuban

Chapter 3 -Sales Funnel Overview:

10 Steps
How To Stop Leaving Money On the Table

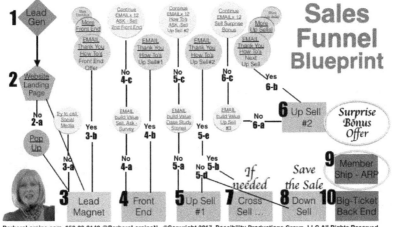

Shameless plug: We offer help with each step of the Sales Funnel, with all the DIY skills you need along the way. And with a team of 20, we offer Done For You services.

Step 1 – Lead Generation. There are many ways to get leads: buying them, advertising, using social media, search engine optimization, networking, giving live presentations, webinars, and more. No matter what method you use, one way or another, lead generation with cost you in money and time.

Part of what you work to accomplish with your Sales Funnel is to get a better ROI from your lead generation efforts. In addition, we seek to give as much value to customers as we can, to serve them with many products, to give customers a better experience - and for you to improve your revenue.

Step 2 – Your Website or Landing Page.

This must be set up to work for you. You must attract attention and make a professional impression with an attractive page.

But that's barely the start. You build interest by showing that you understand people's needs and have the expertise to help; video is the best way to do this. To follow up with people, you need their email address. But . . .

Lead Magnet. Your site visitors expect something in return for their email. That's what your Lead Magnet does.
Video. To do a great job, you should be using short, compelling professional (enough) videos.

Lead Capture Form. Of course, you need a Lead Capture Form that sends contact info directly to your email Service Provider and/or to your Contact Relationship Manager.

Step 3 – Your Lead Magnet.

Not just anything will do to attract visitors to your site and entice them to give you their email. Research your market; learn what appeals to them. Make your Lead Magnet "simply irresistible." Make it *relevant* to them and *valuable*. Big time.

Wow people with your Lead Magnet and you will begin your relationship with them on the right foot. Plus, a great Lead Magnet will give them reasons to share with others how awesome you are. Don't scrimp. Give away your best stuff for free.

It also helps for you to stand out, to be a "Purple Cow," as Seth Godin recommends in his book of the same name. Don't be ordinary – shine!

Survey your social friends, followers, and fans. Use the survey function built into social media platforms or send the survey to your email list. Or use Survey Monkey for free.

Step 2a – If people do not give you their email address, they miss out on the incredible value of your Lead Magnet. Use a "pop up" on your page to further entice people to give a "Yes" and their email address. Yes, I know pop-ups are annoying, but guess what, they get results! So do what works; use a pop-up!

Step 3a - If you still get a "No," know this: without their email, you can't continue to communicate with them. Your opportunities – and theirs - to put your awesomeness to work for them, end there. (If you met them at an event or somewhere other than on your web page, you can call them, they may respond to a phone call or on social media. If you have your address, you can mail to them. The goal is always to get prospects into your email system so you can be, well, systematic (and automatic) with your follow-up.

Step 3b - If they say "Yes" and give you their email, you send them a Thank You email the Download for the Lead Magnet that includes any necessary instructions on how to use the Lead Magnet. You also make your Front End offer, explaining to them how it will augment the value they get from the Lead Magnet. The Thank You email is one of the most over-looked opportunities to make sales, by others. Make sure you use the opportunity to serve and to sell.

Use a video about your Front End product. Add testimonial videos or other social proof. Don't hold back. Remember, this is one of the most important steps – you want them to buy and get into your Sales Funnel.

Obviously, if you are pricing your Front End at $99, you'll have to provide more benefits and proof than if it's priced at $7 or $27. To make sure you product looks like it's worth $99, you can offer big-value bonuses. Since they don't know you yet, they need nudges to get them to the Yes.

It's best for the bonuses to be from your company, but the bonuses could come from the affiliates who are promoting you.

However, you need to be careful at this point, you don't want to have your prospects wander off to another vendor. Even though your affiliates' products don't compete with yours – **you are often competing for prospects' dollars.** So, better to hold off on offering others' product until AFTER your prospect has become your customer.

The "Thank You" email is the first in a series of emails that are designed to guide people through the Sales Funnel, into buying, and buying more and more. How many emails will you need? As many as it takes to achieve maximum ROI from your leads. As Les Brown says, "We won't stop until you win!"

Good copywriting helps. Good script writing for your videos help. (Check out our FREE class on how to come across great on video.)

Step 3c – They are on your email list, but if they did not buy the Front End product. They have not yet made the transition from accepting your free content to becoming a paying customer. (Yikes!) Sell the Front End again. They may not have noticed that offer when you sent them the Thank You for signing up. Do not assume that they are no longer interested
Remember, it can take "12 touches" to get the sale.

Continue emailing them. Send valuable, relevant content. You may want to offer another Front End product. Don't have another one? Create one; then offer that. They signed up for your email; that is proof that they are interested in what you provide. Stick with them and they may buy from you. If you abandon them, you'll never sell them.

Remember Massage Envy and imagine how they thought about what more their customers might want, and that they probably surveyed to ask what they would like.

Step 4 – Your Front End Product. The Front End is mega important. It's the first step your prospects take toward buying, getting into your Sales Funnel, and becoming customers. There are two ways you can go with your Front End. Sell a valuable product with your own marketing and advertising efforts at a "no-brainer" low price, between $7 and $27. Or, develop an even-higher value product that you can have affiliates sell for you at $100. (We'll talk more about pricing later.)

Step 4a – If your site visitor say "no" to your Front End offer, you remind them of the value they get, along with testimonials, social proof, and whatever else it takes to get a yes from them. If they don't respond to with a Yes, you begin the 4c sequence.

Step 4b - After they bought your Front End, you send another Thank You. Like with the Lead Magnet Thank You, you provide instructions on how to use the Front End product. And, you offer the next product. Don't be pushy – serve them, think of what more they might need or want.

Step 4c - If they passed on your Front End, just take a deep breath. Yes, need them to buy your Front End and get into your Sales Funnel. You want to get the party started. And they've said "no thanks." But, remember, it's like Les Brown says, "It's not over until you win." You know that you can absolutely provide the best service, but remember, sometimes it takes 12 touches to get the sale.

Continue sending people helpful emails, provide value, maybe you have another Front End product you can offer them, or you could develop one. Or, when the time is right for them, they might buy a higher-priced product.

Step 5 - Offer your Up Sell #1 If you're already in business, this is your core product. Now that you're thinking in terms of your

Sales Funnel, consider giving your Up Sell #1 offer (and the others that follow) a new look, and maybe a make over. Why?
The goal is to serve your market in the biggest way possible – and for you to reach maximum ROI.

One change you may want to make is to add bonuses to your Up Sell, so that, if they say "No Thanks", you can offer a Down Sell. (See the section on Down Sells.) You may be able to add 10% revenue with a Down Sell offer.

With a sales video, compelling copy, and a "get yours now" button in your email, offer Up Sell #2. Why? You second product is compatible with #1 and odds are they will be very interested. The best time to ask them to buy again is now, while they have just bought. They've already got their credit card out; serve them more with your Up Sell #2.

Like at Massage Envy, now that they are getting a massage they may want those hot rocks – and spend twice as much.
Of course, what that means for you is more revenue, more customer satisfaction, and did I say, more revenue?

Step 5a – If they say No to your Up Sell, you email them, building value, asking what went wrong, and working to sell them. You might share a case study or a story of someone else who's getting big benefits from your Up Sell.

Step 5d – This step might look like it's out of order but it's not. If Step 5a doesn't work, the next step, 5d is to go to the Down Sell.

But, don't go there too quickly, they may have some real reason that they are hesitating. Give them a chance to buy for full price before you go to the Down Sell.

Step 5c – They said No to the Up Sell. Don't give up on them. Ask them what happened, was it that they thought it wasn't direct fit for what they need? If that's the case, offer Up Sell #2 (or other product). Was it the price? If so, maybe they'll go for the Down Sell, or maybe even offer them an additional Front End product. Was it bad timing? Stay in touch with them: build value in your brand: show that you are there to help; be there when the time IS right for them.

5-b - When they buy Up Sell #1, as in *at exactly the time they are ordering* the Up Sell, should you make a Cross Sell Offer?

Amazon increased sales by 35% when they added, their Cross Sell: "people who bought this also bought." Hey, would you like a huge increase in conversions? The Cross Sell might be your golden ticket. It reminds me of the old ad, "Got Milk?" If they don't have milk, they're going to want some for their cereal or with those cookies. (See more in Step 7 about the Cross Sell, below.)

Step 5e – They said Yes to your Up Sell #1. Like with the Lead Magnet and the Front End, you send a Thank You email with how to's for the product. You may want to ask them how the Front End is working for them. The Up Sell #1 they got one of their needs met.

They may (or probably) have more needs that you can be helpful with. So offer them Up Sell #2, You do them a service by providing for more of their needs.

Step 6 – Up Sell #2, #3, and Beyond. Your customers have more than one problem; you should have more than one product so you can solve many of their problems. Each Up Sell is a fit with the ones that went before. You build your business – and your Sales Funnel – to serve your niche.

Step 6a - If they said No to the Up Sell #2, send them an email thanking them for being a customer, build value, be at their service, and offer Up Sell #3.

Step 6c – If they said no to your Up Sell #2, continue emailing them helpful information. You may want to begin offering the Surprise Bonus.

Your Surprise Bonus Offer – Your Membership. After your customer has bought your Up Sell (or even after you sell the Lead Magnet), you can begin offering your Membership. Why? Because it will give them enormous value, sell them on your other Up Sells (because they will feel there are topics they are missing out on), and you will enjoy Automatic Recurring Payments.

Just think what this means, even as you are beginning your Membership, let's say your Membership will be $50 a month, but you make a 50% off "Introductory offer," with just 100 members, that's $2,500 a month. And when you can switch to the full $50 a month, that's $5,000 a month – automatically recurring. Yeah.

Step 7 - Do Your Customers Need a Cross Sell Product?
Remember, these are products that a person might need with their Up Sell. For example, at Radio Shack they ask if you need batteries. For this program, it could be, "Videos are so important, do you need our tips on DIY videos." At Massage Envy it is, "Would you like the Aroma Therapy with your massage?"

If they say "Yes" to the Cross Sell, you make more money. If they say "no," at least they know that you tried to be helpful with something they might need or want. (Later you'll learn that you can make 35% more by using a Cross Sell.)

Step 8 – The Down Sell is designed to salvage a sale that is just not going to happen. You've given the sales process your best shot, but they are ready to walk away. At this point, you offer them a lower price for a striped-down version of your Up Sell.

The thing is if the buyer didn't value the extra features included in your Up Sell, they'd rather have the lower price. And you'd rather have 80% of the original price instead of a big fat zero.

Step 9 – This is your Membership Back End product. This is designed to give ongoing value to your members and automatic recurring payments to you. The other plus is that, your participating members, will become more aware of the products and services you offer, and discover that they really do want them. Cha ching! So, your members are probably your best customers; take extra-good care of them.

Step 10 – The big-ticket Back End is where you can make really big bucks from each client. No matter what it is that they bought, give them stellar service. And, since what they wanted was elite, exclusive, VIP treatment, constantly look for ways to give them that extraordinary treatment.

Don't find customers for your products.
Find products for your customers.

- Seth Godin

What it costs to operate your Sales Funnel:

- Lead Generation (LinkedIn $50/month, Twitter $12/month, on-line ads, publicity . . .)
- Website & Landing Pages (1 per product)
- Lead Magnet Product (Use more creativity than cash)
- Email Provider with Auto-Responder (Mail Chimp - $10/month for 500)
- Front End Product (With value of $7 - $27 OR make it Affiliate-Ready with $100 value)
- Email Sales Letter Campaigns for Each Step of the Funnel
- Up Sell #1 Product (Create or Re-Think Your Product)
- Cross Sell Products (What do people need to go along with your Up Sells. Provide it yourself or Joint Venture)
- Up Sell #2, #3 . . . (What additional products do your market need, that you "should" provide.* Provide them yourself or Joint Venture. How many products? How many solutions are relevant to your market?
- Down Sell (Plan your offers so that you can offer at a lower price by giving them less)
- Membership Back End (Point all your prospects and clients toward becoming Members. It may work instead of Front End, or at any point in the Sales Funnel. Think: Automatic Recurring Payments, and try to wipe the smile off your face.
- Big-Ticket Back End (Build your "celebrity" to prepare for offering a big bucks solution)

BarbaraLoraine.com 858-231-3140 @BarbaraLoraineN
Barbara@BarbaraLoraine.com Facebook.com/BarbaraLoraineBiz

Climbing to the top of

Mt. Everest is exhilarating.

It's the same when you are climbing

to reach the peak in your business.

- Werner Berger

Chapter 4 - Know Your Numbers

When you understand the numbers involved in your marketing and sales activities, you can make better predictions and decisions. Following are some of important numbers and concepts.

Cost Per Lead and ROI
To determine your cost per lead (CPL), divide the total advertising dollars spent by the number of leads that came in and you have your cost per lead.

Example: You have a company that did 31 jobs for a total of $389,529 in sales over the last 12 months. You had 124 calls in for estimates, or leads. You spent $13,750 on advertising. Dividing $13,640 by 124 we get a cost of $110 per lead.

How does that information help us? Try this. If you want to increase your sales this year to $500,000, how can you do it?

Lets say that last year you sold 31 jobs for a total of $389,529 in sales, resulting in an average job size of $12,565. Assuming the job size will remain unchanged, to reach $500,000 next year you need to sell 40 jobs ($500,000 / $12,565).

You know that you sold 31 jobs out of 124 leads last year, for a sales ratio of 1 in 4. To sell 40 jobs this year, you'll need 160 leads, an increase of 36 leads.

Focus on ROI From Customer Retention

According to Jenny Vance, President of Lead Jen, instead of asking about Cost Per Lead, the real question marketers should focus on is if they are hitting their revenue goals. By shifting the goals of marketing to align with revenue instead of the number of leads, the number of leads doesn't much matter as long as revenue numbers are reached.

This is a different approach that focuses more on customer experience and retention than lead generation.
The Sales Funnel helps improve ROI, customer experience, and retention because customers are given more of the solutions and fulfilling experiences they seek.

Customer Lifetime Value

This calculation seeks to predict the value of the future relationship with a customer. This information encourages marketers to shift their focus from strictly building sales to fostering positive relationships. Because it is forward looking, CLV can be useful in shaping managers' decisions but is much more difficult to quantify. While quantifying Customer Profitability (CP) is a matter of carefully reporting and summarizing the results of past activity, quantifying CLV involves forecasting future activity.

To Calculate CLV, use the following formula.

$$CLV = ((T \ x \ AOV) \ AGM) \ \text{ALT}$$

Where:

T = Average monthly transactions

AOV = Average order value

ALT = Average Customer Lifespan (in months)

AGM = Average gross margin

Following Is An Example To Calculate Your Customer Lifetime Value

Let's assume the following:

- Profit generated by the customer each year = $1,000
- Number of years that they are a customer of the brand = 5 years
- Cost to acquire the customer = $2,000

The customer lifetime value of this customer would be:

$1,000 (annual profit from the customer) X

5 (number of years that they are a customer) less

$2,000 (acquisition cost) = $3,000 = CLV.

That is, $1,000 X 5 – $2,000 = $3,000.

Again, the Sales Funnel can improve your CLV by encouraging new product development and new opportunities for earnings. You can improve your CLV by offering new Up Line products, Cross Sells, and Down Sells.

It's not enough to direct traffic to your site or to get them to give you their email address with your Lead Magnet product. What you need to do is create products and offers that give clients what they want - in the way (and at the prices) they want it. The Sales Funnel makes the most of your traffic, leads, and products, by focusing on serving your clients the products and services they need, want, and will pay for.

There's another way to look at these costs though. Companies that only track leads (Cost per Lead) and not conversion to sales (Cost Per Sale) are making a big mistake. That is because many times, a low cost per lead does not mean a low cost per sale. Low cost leads often do not convert as well to sales. What matters is Cost Per Sale and whether you are making a profit (from sales) from a particular lead source.

The number you should base your decisions on is this: "If I spend a dollar on this advertising, how much money will I get back over the lifetime of this customer?" It is the dollars that matter, not the percentages. You can't spend percentages at the grocery store or deposit them in the bank.

Make sure you have a clear understanding of your sales sequence and how your Front End and Back End campaigns are tied together.

It's not about having the right opportunities.
It's about handling the opportunities right.

- Mark Hunter

Chapter 5 – Lean Lead Generation

Low cost lead generation makes easier for lean startups to get the prospects they need, get them into the Sales Funnel, and turn them into customers why buy over and over again.

This is not a book about Lead Generation. But the subject is so important, and for many start ups doing lead generation in a cost effective way is key to their success – so I thought 'd weigh in on some of the lowest cost ways to get leads and clients.

Of course, Social Media channels can be great low cost or free sources of leads. Some are better than others, in my opinion.

Before sharing my ideas, please know that the following ideas are not definitive, and they are very situational. What might be perfect for someone else's business goals might be a total waste of limited money for you. Having made those statements, lets take a look at how Social Media can work for you.

Be respectful of the channel. When using any social media, become familiar with the platform's terms of service and be respectful of the free opportunity they provide and of the channel's community in general.

Put others first. Don't be on social media trolling for dollars. Look to serve others. People want to be entertained, inspired, and informed – in other words they want you to give them value. People do not log onto social media so you can sell them. That's a huge turn off. Serve; don't sell. Give; don't take. I've thought long and hard about what "gift" to give people who follow, subscribe, like, or share my content.

Sometimes, to receive my gift, I do not require an email address from my social media peeps. After that first strong connection, then I'll ask for an email. An email address and willingness to accept future messages is a lot for people to give. People giving you their email are a big price for them to pay for your free offer. Be respectful.

You should think of ways for you to best serve others. Take a longer-term approach; it will pay off. Remember what Gary V says, "Give, give and then ask."

After having said all that, social media is a great place to engage, and to give first. Most don't do that though, they go right into trying to sell you something, or they never try to find out if they can serve you at all.

You can most definitely use social media channels for lead generation, but there's a way to do it. (I'll be blogging about that, or even doing a video. Watch for that on my website, **http://BarbaraLoraine.com**)

Know This: For newbies, once you've decided on which market to target into, you can use social media to make connections with the people that are already in the market, especially the leaders. But always find the "what's in it for them."

Facebook

First let's talk about Facebook. Facebook is mega-attractive because of the shear numbers of members and the potential for engagement. However, on Facebook, you can only communicate with people who are either friends or fans. And Facebook does not serve up your posts to your entire group of friends or fans. So, opportunities for lead generation are limited to your already-existing groups and to how many of them Facebook is showing your content to.

Advertising on Facebook can be very productive, but it's not free.

It can be very cost-effective, so look into how you may be able to use it for generating leads. Facebook seems to be particularly helpful for attracting attendees to events. I have often gotten an invitation and passed it on to many others directly and by posting it on my page. You may be surprised at how affordable Facebook can be, so check it out.

Twitter
I love Twitter for lead generation and building awesome connections. First, you can build your list by simply following other people who are a fit for your business. A part of what it takes to encourage people to follow you back is that you like and re-tweet other's posts and that you post content that others will like and re-tweet. So, of course, you must post great content.

Twitter closes the

six degrees of separation

to one degree of separation.

-   Gary Vaynerchuk

When we first started using Twitter at our office, we didn't have time or resources to create articles and other informational content - especially not 20 or 30 times a day! But what we could do all day every day is to post inspirational content. I often get 20 to 50 likes AND re-tweets of my inspirational posts. And it's been typical for me to attract around 1,000 new followers each week.

I often get a chuckle out of what does get shared and what doesn't. One of my messages that said, The best time to plant a tree is 20 years ago; the second best time is now" with a Gif of Snoop Dog nodding and saying "Agreed," it immediately got lots of 48 likes and 29 re-tweets. But the message that said, "You grow your business and your business grows you," with a Gif of Tyler Perry as Madea, saying "Hell to the yeah!" got just four likes and no re-tweets. Sorry Tyler, America thinks you're awesome, but in my business-oriented Twitter posts, I guess not so much.

LinkedIn. LinkedIn was made for business connections. While it first served job seekers it is the best for creating business interactions. While you can use the free service to connect with people, first you have to join groups, and then communicate with your 2nd Level plus contacts. For $49 a month, you can send a direct message to anyone you want to meet. That is a huge bang for your buck. Yes, "Free is always in the budget," but sometimes it's just smarter and more cost effective to pay the price.

Google AdWords

Yes, Google AdWords can be expensive. Sometimes it costs more to not get in front of your prospects, though. You might want to give Google AdWords or other online ads a try, and then weigh the cost of ads against what you actually gain. But . . .

Really look at the opportunities with retargeting ads. When you have already attracted attention on Facebook, Twitter, and/or LinkedIn, and attracted visitors to your website, you can "follow" those prospects with retargeting ads.

Just in case you don't know what retargeting is, it's those ads you see when you've visited a website and then, as you continue surfing the net, you'll see ads from the site you just visited. The payoff for retargeting ads can be immense, so check them out.

Related to Sales Funnel and the process it includes, are Customer Relationship Management and email service providers for your campaigns and auto-responders, so I'll mention them here. Small business people often like to operate "out of a shoe box" in many ways, with bookkeeping and with keeping track of leads and the sales process. Don't do that. You must use a CRM or you will have prospects, leads, and clients slip through the cracks.

Find out what people want
. . . and give them that.

-Anonymous

Chapter 6 – Making Sales

What does it take for someone to buy? I'm not going to talk here about salesmanship, that's a broad subject. And it's not my subject. We like sales trainers that teach with the "serving not selling" style that gives value to prospects and generates sales for the business

When it comes to making sales, we hear a lot about how many "touches" (or exposures to a brand) are required before people buy.

According to the Business Insider, "In the case of an impulse purchase, only one contact is needed, but this usually happens inside a favorite store where there is already a level of confidence and trust, or the price is so low that it does not matter to the buyer."

Give people the 5 – 12 "touches" they need to get to the "Yes." The following images shows Microsoft's report on what happens at the time of each touch.

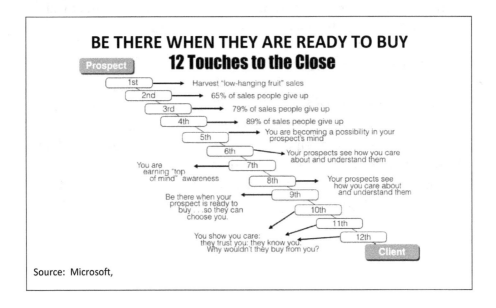

Source: Microsoft,

It's a fact: consumers want convenient shopping. They don't want to search high and low for the best providers. They want you to provide them with the proof and the follow through that convinces them they should choose you. Further, once they have heard about you, they don't want to have to remember who you are. They want they want you to be there, easily accessible, when they are ready to buy.

Give people the 5 – 12 "touches" they need to get to the "Yes." The following images shows Microsoft's report on what happens at the time of each touch.

How many touches does it take?

Business Insider asked, "How many touches are required on average before the sale? In the case of an impulse purchase, only one contact is needed, but this usually happens inside a favorite store where there is already a level of confidence and trust, or the price is so low that it does not matter to the buyer."

"Research suggests that three touches are needed; or is it five, or eight, or twelve? The only right answer is "it depends." But, following a schedule and maximizing the value of each contact will decrease the time, effort and total cost of each sale."

Why so many touches?

According to the **Online Marketing Institute**, one reason it takes a multitude of touches to generate a sales-ready lead is the sheer amount of information required to deem a lead sales-ready: Budget, Authority, Need, and Timeline. Understanding what this information means for your company, and having the appropriate number of interactions with prospects to determine sales-readiness is key.

As you look at the image chart on the previous page, notice the needs that "touches" fulfill during the follow-up process. With each touch, you build more familiarity, along with feelings of trust, belief, and comfort with you, Buyers need that comfort in order to choose you.

Notice in the image chart that most salespeople just pick up the "low hanging fruit" of those who buy right away. And 62% don't bother to make a second contact. Seventy-nine percent give up after the third contact. Yet people become more ready to buy after 6, 8, or even 12 contacts. Yikes.

Look at the chart and also notice that, as the salesperson's attention can wane, the prospects' interest in buy from you can increase – a lot.

Your prospect's interest in buying increases, but if you are no longer anywhere in site, they won't be buying from you!

Now, consider that not all people are just browsing Lookie Lou's; some are seriously ready to buy. The thing is, those people will buy . . . somewhere, from someone. You can set the odds in your favor of you getting the sale by following up and staying in touch.

This is why automating your sales follow-up and tracking process is so important. That's what a Contract Relationship Management platform does.

Contact Relationship Management (CRM). Prices for CRMs range from $10 a month for Less Annoying CRM, to $60 a month for Sales Force, and $300 a month for Infusion Soft. Check them out see which fits you best. Do yourself a favor. Don't miss out by not staying on track.

Email Campaign Platform with Auto-Responder. In addition to tracking sales and automating the Sales Funnel, an email campaign platform – with auto-responder capacity – is mandatory.

I like Mail Chimp. A lot of people choose Mail Chimp because it's absolutely free forever for up to 2,000 contacts. That's very generous. But you must use an auto-responder feature, and with Mail Chimp that is $10 a month.

I've heard people say that you can do follow-up emails with a free Mail Chimp account. Doing one follow-up email will not be good enough for running your sales funnel. You need to do multiple follow-up and sales emails that are set on automatic. Period. It's $10; don't miss out for the sake of saving $10 a month.

There are many email providers. As you are shopping, be sure to choose one with an auto-responder feature – auto-responders are an important part of your Sales Funnel. (As a side note, the other thing i like about Mail Chimp is that it synchs well with other programs, like CRMs, Word Press and more.)

If you're *interested*, you will do what is convenient. If you're *committed*, you will do whatever it takes.

- John Assaraf

Chapter 7 – Sales Funnel, a Closer Look

After knowing why you need to implement the sales funnel in your business, it is time to understand the ingredients of the Sales Funnel and the role each element is designed to perform. We'll first outline the process, then we'll talk about each element in some depth with examples. Later in the book we'll look at how to create your Sales Funnel Products.

The Sales Funnel organizes your system, plans for the additional products, and offers that increase your revenue. It also anticipates the needs and wants of buyers. Here is the formula:

The Sales Funnel - Products

Lead Magnet	Front End	UpSell #1	Cross Sell
Down Sell	UpSell #2	UpSell #3	Back End

Now let's look at each element and consider the roles each must perform. Later, we'll provide examples of each type of product.

1 - The Lead Magnet Offer

This is your main lead generation tool. What you want to end up with is your prospect's contact information so you can build a relationship with them, serve them with your products and services, and make revenue.

The Lead Magnet is usually free and you use it to "trade" value with your prospect. That want information (or some other value) that you have. You want access to them through your emails – and your Sales Funnel.

Even though this product is free, you should create a perception of great value with it. It should be considered a real gift. It should make people happy to have said "Yes" to giving you their email – and make them want to continuing receiving your emails.

Give big value. Give more than you think you should. It is counter-intuitive; you think that if you give so much for free, they'll feel they can just do it themselves and they won't need to buy from you. Realize this: you are giving them value *and* they are giving you their *email address*. . . and an opportunity to sell them later. They are giving you a "gift" just as much as you are with them. Do not underestimate the importance of getting into their awareness in a positive way.

Besides, many of your subscribers will not be "do it yourselfers." Once they feel the need for what you offer, how they can benefit from your services, and the ROI then can expect - they become serious prospects . . . and buyers of your training or done for you services. . .

With a great Lead Magnet, you build credibility, trust, and feelings of confidence in what more you can provide.

Lead Magnet - Here's a big corporate Service/Online Example
Google – Lead Magnet: free search engine service, plus free maps, and much more. The free stuff from Google goes on and on. What do they get from that? They earn extreme good will and loyalty. In addition to that, brands see the ads, feel good about Google, and become interested in advertising.

Retargeting ads follow a consumer around. People visit a site and consume information. Next time they do a Google search, they see the ad of the site they just visited. These "touches" are often highly effective at turning prospect's interest into buying action.

Of course Google is an extreme example of a Lead Magnet give away.

Let's look at other more mainstream examples.

- Attorneys, CPAs, and other consultants give a free 30-minute consultation. If the visitor feels good about them, they will hire them.

- Professionals give free presentations – sometimes even including a meal. That's why we talked before about the value of a client and the client's lifetime value. You must know those numbers in deciding what you can invest in Lead Magnet offers.

- Dentists give free exams or even teeth whitening, which brings patients in for exams and other dental work.

- In fact Ulta Beauty and Sephora Shops are great examples of Lead Magnet. The Sephora stores are party-like atmospheres with free samples of perfume and products freely offered, and greatly appreciated. On the other hand, Ulta Beauty offers rewards points, which according to an online review "really add up and you redeem them for actual money off of your purchase, including prestige brands. Plus they have 2x-5x point bonuses for specific brands fairly often, which are great too."

These are examples of Lead Magnets and the "Rule of Reciprocity" in action. The gals shopping at Ulta receive a "gift" of a perfume sample and more. The shop's visitors feel cared about, and are inclined to purchase from Ulta – even though they can buy more cheaply elsewhere or online.

Indeed, Ulta is a great example of the successful retail store model of today. Don't just sell merchandise, but offer an experience that gets shoppers off the Internet and into their stores.

Other stores, like Macy's and Penney's, have not been so responsive to what consumers want now. Those stores, and their troubles, have been in the news because, in the world on online shopping bargains and convenience, brick and mortar stores are in danger and trying to find ways to survive.

"Evergreen" Products

As you are planning to build your Lead Magnet (or any of the other products), plan for it to be "**evergreen**." Being evergreen means it will appeal to many people, because the market is vast and promises to fulfill needs that will last for a very long time. It also means that it will appeal over time.

For instance, in my Sales Funnel work, lead generation methods, how to build Lead Magnets, and how to produce DIY videos are recurring, "evergreen" topics. Regardless of what kind of business people are in, they will definitely need to get visitors to their website, subscribers to their email, and buyers for their products.

In later chapters, we will talk at length about how to develop your Lead Magnet.

Distrust and skepticism created during the Great Recession changed how people buy. People like to get something for nothing up front – before they spend. So the old saying, "You get what you pay for went out the window." So did the saying, "If it's too good to be true, it probably is." Consider the enormous value we get these days for free. GPS, YouTube, Google search, Facebook, Twitter, apps galore – all free. There might not be a "free lunch," but we do get lots of free stuff.

When people give their email in exchange for a Lead Magnet offer, they expect what they receive to be great! And, to reduce risk, these days people like one-step-at-a-time purchases.

When a consumer derives value - especially from something that was given for free - he becomes the best kind of evangelist.

- William James

2 - Front End **Product**

The Front End Product is one of the most important elements of the Sales Funnel. With the first offer, you acquired the lead's contact information (usually just their email address). Now the job of the Front End Product is to nudge the prospect into becoming a buyer. This product must entice the visitor to click the "Buy Now," button, take out their credit card, and make a purchase.

The Front- End product is usually low priced. The price is supposed to be such a "no brainer," that it's easy for the person to buy. I remember buying a product recently that I actually thought, "Hey, if it's no good, it's only $10. I'll go for it." You want to make it easy peasy for a person to become a buyer and to take the very important step into your Sales Funnel.

By making even a small purchase, the buyer shows that they will take out their credit card and buy. They also prove that they are interested in the subject of your product, and may (or probably) will be interested in more of the products you offer. That's all very good news. However . . .

The Front End product is *not* a source of profits for the business. It's what they call in retail stores a "loss leader," which is a way to get people into the store, where the merchant can entice shoppers into buying more.

With the Front End product, people get to see what your "real" (not free) products are like, including your customer experience, and service if they have a problem.

To say it a different way, the Front End product is characterized by a no-brainer price (usually from $7 to $47, we'll talk more about these prices later) for a high-value product. This paid-for product gives the customer a chance to really get to know you and how you will perform for them. Wow! them with value and they'll feel more certain that, as you offer your higher-priced products, they can count on getting even more value.

The Front End product may be your most important. Don't think less of your Front End products because of their low cost – they perform an important job. Your Front End product encourages prospects to turn into buyers . . . and to step into your Sales Funnel, where your greater income opportunities reside.

When it comes to Internet Marketing examples, I'll use my own sales funnel as an example. Once someone has consumed my freebie (I offer a variety of offers that I rotate to hit more people's needs and wants, and offer different offers for different market segments), they

get my Front End offer, with one of my products designed to give big value at a small price. As an example, I offer a Sales Funnel Planner Session, with a $250 value for just $47 to $100. (In the section on building your products, I'll discuss this price issue more.)

After they have used that product I can make the up-sell offer of one of my main moneymaking programs, for example, Sales Funnel for DIY Success. In that program, for just $250, clients get hands-on and actually create their Sales Funnel. We kick around ideas for your Lead Magnet, and trip wire product because many companies don't have these and it's hard for them to think of what they might develop to get prospects into the Sales Funnel. This program is an extraordinary value. Plus it leads into to our other training programs, and products.

I'm not sharing my Funnel with you to sell you, but to impress upon you that Sales Funnels work for all kinds of businesses and are designed to create extreme ROI.

As an example of a retail Front End product, we'll talk about Lush. At the Lush Store they demonstrate their "Honey Bath Bomb." As they say, "You get into a hot bath after a long day and just drop in the bomb." The bomb "explodes" with color and moisture swirling into the water, while the fragrance eases away the cares of the day and transports you into luxurious relaxation." With prices starting at just $5, Lush creates an addictive allure for consumers.

What Front End product can you use to encourage people to take the first step and become a buyer?

3 – Up Sell 1, 2, 3 and ...

Once you know what your prospects and customers are interested in, develop product for them. And then ... come up with more products. Keep selling to the people who already bought until 1) you don't get any response to a product, or 2) you retire to the South of France, or where floats your boat.

You'll make plenty of money with your Sales Funnel, especially with your Up Sell, Cross Sell, and Back End productions.

If your customer bought a book on the Front End, you could offer a workbook, audio files, online course or videos as complements to the book. Each of your offers should enhance the value of the product they just purchased.

Once you realize that you don't need to make money on the Front End, then you can feel better about investing to bring in a lot more customers for the Up Sell. The amount of names you can mail to grows exponentially.

You might be saying – "But I don't have any additional products to sell." Which raises an important question: How do you come up with additional products to sell?

Think in terms of a product LINE instead of just one product. Every product line can be expanded. Consider that an information product can be made into a series of seven products or more:

1. Initial "beginner/introductory" course

2. Advanced course

3. DVD of live seminar

4. Live Seminar in Person

5. Monthly newsletter or membership site

6. Group coaching/mastermind groups

7. Personalized coaching from the guru

These are the products where your business starts – and continues - making real money. These are logical, helpful add-ons to the Front End product.

The Front End is so low cost that buyers are not surprised that they need more to give them a full solution to their problem. And, clients are not surprised that the Up-Sell costs more than the Front End product.

After all, while consumers love the bargain price of the Front End, they know that no business could survive by making such little money by giving such big value. For the business, this is good news because, now that the client has experienced the Front End and the first Up Sell, they are ready for more.

It goes without saying, but we'll say it anyhow because it's crucial to your success, all your products should be world class, deliver huge value, and leave clients saying, "Wow!"

The success of your Sales Funnel rests on you having incredible products. No amount of great sales copy and follow-up will matter if your products suck. So make sure your products are awesome. Further, your success depends on you having several products. It's like Josh Godin said in the quote we shared earlier, "find more products to present to you customers."

You're awesome, so people want to buy more awesomeness from you. And we can't forget the little detail: you want to make as much money as possible from your client and prospect list.

Up Sell Products 1, 2, 3, 4, 5 . . . These are products that solve additional, bigger problems; they are necessary for your clients. As another example, we'll use McDonalds. If you order just a burger, you can expect to hear, "Do you want fries and a drink with that? In fact, no matter what you order, they will offer another Up Sell.
When it comes to their signature products, their burgers, McDonalds is not so profitable.

The Up Sell products are where *you* will probably make most of your income, but it isn't that way for McDonalds. Up Sells are your usually your bread and butter. But that also doesn't mean that all of your Up Sells provide your best profit margin.

How Many Up Sells?
In our Sales Funnel Blueprint chart, we show the Up Sell happening three times. But there could be just one Up Sell, like with Neil Patel's Advanced Internet Marketing program. He goes from giving free articles on his blog and a free webinar, straight to selling a pricey program.

Patel has no Front End pricing at all, he goes straight to the Up Sell. Of course, in his case, this is not his only income stream, he's founder of KISSmetrics, Hello Bar, and Crazy Egg. As a consultant, he helps companies like Amazon, NBC, GM, HP and Viacom grow their revenue. So don't worry about Neil, he's doing just fine with his one Up Sell product.

Let's look at Massage Envy as an example of a fully-built out well-functioning Sales Funnel. As of this writing, as their Front End, they are running a special (for first time customers only, and at limited locations) of $50 price on a one-hour massage (normally $99) or facial (usually $109)

Massage Envy offers a full range of services massage and skin care services, I'll share a few prices here to illustrate the Sales Funnel. As I said, a basic 60-minute massage is $99. As a nice Up Sell, they offer a massage with hot rocks for $199. Their Cross Sells (which we will talk about in a bit) include a Sugar Scrub or Aroma Therapy with the massage for an additional $15 or they also offer facials Deep Muscle Massage (which is, well, a deeper pressure during the massage) for an additional $18.

But here's where Massage Envy really shines – with their membership. Again, as of this writing, for $59 a month you get a one-hour basic massage. Prices for additional massages and for add-on services (or facials), are offered at very reduced prices.

We'll talk more later about how a Membership can really expand customer loyalty – and your income.

At our company, when we do a website for a client (which includes a promo video) we ask:

- "Do you also want an 'about us' page video, an 'explainer' video?" Or,
- "Would you like to learn how to produce your own videos, with our training?" Or,
- "Do you need help with you email campaigns and auto-responder or help with your Lead Magnet – or other products?"

No matter where a client starts with us – we can serve – and Up Sell or Cross Sell them with many other products.

You can discover opportunities for additional Up Sell products and Cross Sell products by forecasting problems or needs that your clients will probably face.

Evergreen, Revisited

Staples has an interesting, evergreen category in its Sales Funnel. It's reported that, 20% of their revenue comes from ink. Twenty percent! With a store full of supplies, furnishings, and equipment, ink is the biggest seller. So, they want people to buy printers and to print. Ink is an "evergreen" Cross Sell product that keeps people coming back, and provides Staples with secure, regular income.

Consider the success of Michael Dubin, founder of Dollar Shave Club.
He saw the need for better razors at lower prices, produced a viral-worthy video, set up an auto-ship membership sales model – and the rest is history.

In your business, think what consumables or evergreen product needs there could be? What would it take to build that Cross Sell or Up Sell into your Sales Funnel?

For us, we will be offering a Membership with exclusive training, coaching, and masterminding. This will be a high-value experience only available to members. Membership can be a win-win, evergreen addition to your Sales Funnel.

Here are some brick & mortar Up Sell and Cross Sell examples:

- **Car dealerships sell you service and oil changes.** Services are very high-profit. The send regular emails as a "courtesy reminders" to their customers of scheduled maintenance.

- **TV show hosts start a magazine and sell their branded products.** Rachel Ray is a perfect example. Ray built a market on TV. Now she offers, cookware, a magazine, and even dog food. When they love you, they want to buy more from you.

- **Oprah's products are her "O Magazine,"** programming, and her OWN network. Oprah also produces shows like Rachel Ray, Dr. Phil, and Dr. Oz, to add to her income.

- **Theaters sell you food and beverages.** The concession stands are an important source of revenue for theaters (and all entertainment venues). Now some theaters provide pizza and even dinner served at VIP dinner tables.

- **Electronics stores sell you warranties.** Since warranties are seldom used, this is almost all profit for the stores.

As we said earlier, Front End products open the buying loop. The **Up** Sells and are the main sources of your revenue. Some Up Sells are higher priced, some aren't. Some are one-time purchases; some are evergreen.

In many cases, you can offer the Up Sell immediately after people buy your Front End product. In other situations, you use emails to stay front- of-mind, and offer product when the consumer is ready to buy.
What more do your customers need and want from you? Can you add an auto-ship option or Membership to your list of Up Sell offers?

4 – Your Cross Sell Product

These products, like the Up Sell, are a natural fit or compatible with the Front End products. They can also be good add-ons to Up Sell products. They add more income for you, as you'll clearly see when we get into examples later on. We say, "Mo' income is just mo' better."

The Cross Sell is a companion to the Up Sell. (In fact, it could be considered an Up Sell, so don't get hung up on the name.) The Cross Sell is great for buyers to have at the same time as the Up Sell. The Cross Sell is similar to the Up-Sell Product but feels a little different.

It's often a companion product instead of a product that stands alone.

McDonalds is a perfect example of a physical product Cross Sell. "Do you want fries with that? How about a drink?" (Of course, you might also call this an Up-Sell.) You see, McDonalds doesn't make much from their burgers, but from the fries and drinks they have huge profit margins. For the customer, it seems like they are getting a great deal when they are given a "bundle" price that includes the burger, fries and drink.

At the car wash, you can get a basic wash or you can go for the Cross-Sell of getting your car waxed, or your tires, given special attention.
And in the shop at the car wash, you can get fragrance for your car, a cup of coffee, get your shoes shined, and even a greeting card to send
to your sweetie. All of these products add to profits – and provide convenience for the buyer.

At the nail salon, when you order a manicure, you are automatically offered a pedicure.

Amazon does a great job with the cross sell. Once you are making your purchase Amazon shows you that "others also bought _____ (similar product), when they bought what you are about to buy."

When to Use the Cross Sell?
The best time to sell is right when people are already buying. Sell the fries with that burger. Sell wax with the car wash. Sell shoes to go with the dress on Amazon. "People who bought this also bought…"

When it comes to service products, we can offer additional programs, like with a website program, we can offer how to do your own videos. Our marketing clients are going to need a video – or several. Videos are expensive to have produced, so we offer DIY training. Offering this program is good for our bottom line and a great service for our clients.

With the Cross Sell, you can improve your overall profit margins a lot. When someone buys from you, that's the best time to offer an additional, add-on (cross sell), or another up sell. It's not all about your profits, though. The fact is that the client who benefits by making one purchase from you will benefit even more by buying, well, more.

Note: You don't leave anything out of the Front-Line or Up-Sell offer in order to force a sale of the next product. Instead, it is an additional, upgraded product, something the clients needs and/or want and will benefit from in an even bigger way than if they purchased just one product.

When it comes to the Cross Sell, while this technique increases profits, it also solidifies the relationship with the client.
At the tire store, if you get an email reminding you to rotate your tires, customers appreciate that. And when they come in for to have their tires rotated, the mechanic may find more work that needs to be done on the car.

Some auto-maintenance shops offer a free tire rotation with an oil change. That's why we said earlier that it's important to know your numbers. What does it cost to do the free tire rotation? Offering free services is great, but only if the numbers work.

Here's an example of an online service product:
Suppose you sell web design services. Many clients will not know how to promote or use search engine optimization. So you could cross-sell these consulting services (either by providing them yourself, or by creating a partnership with a company that will provide them for you).

When it comes to your Sales Funnel, products are the foundation. Need more or a different look at your products? We can help. That's one of our Cross Sells. Similarly, if you've got products and not a well organized, results-producing Sales Funnel, we can help. And that's another Cross Sell.

Other Opportunities
If you don't have product that your market wants, you can Joint Venture (JV) with a company that does. Then, you can offer the product to your buyers when they want it, while they are making their purchase with you. We'll talk more about this later. This is a win-win-win for you, your customers and your JV partners.

5 – How to Down Sell

The Down Sell salvages deals that might otherwise not work out. These are "better than nothing" deals that can add 10% to your overall income. That's nothing to sneeze at.
What's the Down Sell? If (or when) your prospect is not saying "Yes," you're about to lose the sale. You can make the purchase a smaller step; offer a smaller piece of the product, or a "starter kit" price.

You see the Down Sell in all industries. Consider the travel business. You know you want to go to Paris, but with the five star hotels, you're over budget. The travel agent can ask: "Which are more important to you, dining out and attractions, or the room? . . . If the attractions are most important, you can still have your Paris dreams come true. Why don't we schedule you for a lower-priced room?"

Car dealers Down Sell all the time. If you enter a dealership looking for a BMW and get scared off by the price, the salesman will certainly bring up many other options that cost less. That is Down Selling.

We've done this before with marketing clients who are worried about buying into a pricey marketing package that includes all the solutions they need. We may say, "Just get your toe into the water with just a landing page so you can check out what it's like to work with us." Or it could be, "Why don't you start with just 20% of the price upfront, instead of the usual 50% - let's just get you started, so you can start seeing benefits."

A version of the Down Sell is offering pricing concessions. Maybe your product is $1,200, but buyers would prefer payments. You can offer a full price of $1,000 paid upfront or payments of $100 dollars a month for a year. Essentially, you make it possible for people to buy the way that works best for them.

On the Internet, there's another kind of down sell. This was inspired by ecommerce sites, where shopping carts are often abandoned. The site owner worked to get the prospect to their site, to make an attractive offer, and to entice the prospect to make a purchase . . . almost.

As an example, plus-size clothier, Jessica London offers a choice of Down Sells:

- 40% off 2 items
- First 2 40% off with 3
- First 3 40% off with 30% off other items

Once you browse Jessica London's site and put an item in the shopping cart, if you start to leave the site, they come back with another offer: "How about free shipping and 15% off?"
As already stated, the Down Sell salvages a deal that otherwise wouldn't happen. There's money on the table that's about to disappear, so you make another offer to sweeten the deal. This is a win-win . . .Unless shoppers know that the discount is a possibility and *always* hold out for the lower price offer.

6 – Back End

Usually, back end sales are where you can earn a lot of money. Because they are already customers, you don't incur advertising expense other than sending out emails.

With the Back End, you offer products to people who have already bought from you. They trust you, and they have money. Not only that, you offer products that are designed to enhance the value from a product your customer already purchased. Please note: your Back End product must be related to your main product.

Some Back End products are your big-ticket offers. Some are "evergreen" products they will buy over time. (More on this later.) The high-end products are not for all your prospects or clients. They are VIP service and exclusive. They are premium quality at a premium price. They are the profit maximizers of your Sales Funnel. The fact is, some people want to spend a lot of money to get V. I. P. treatment, special access, or exclusive offers. They *want* to pay more that fits their self-image. Why not let them?

If your customer bought a book, you could offer a workbook, audio files, online course or videos as complements to the book. Each of your offers should be a complement or enhance the value of the product they just purchased.

What Back End products have you bought?

- First class airline seats
- VIP passes at events
- VIP rooms in nightclubs
- Full day, one-on-one consulting
- Platinum Membership
- High-end spa services
- Other

Notice that you *want* to buy a VIP experience. You can't be sold into it with strong arm tactics. Some people simply want the exclusive offering.

The good news is, Back End products maximize the profits and ROI from your Sales Funnel. These products can require some creativity to develop but they supply enormous profits.

Usually the Backend product is the product with the highest price among the other offers in the Sales Funnel, but not always, as you'll see in the upcoming chapter on how to build your Back End.
Gain people's trust before you offer them the Backend, this is the key to closing your Backend offer sales.

You may want to mention your back end product during the promotions of your Front End and Up Sell products. You could say, "One of my one-on-one clients, who flew in from London to spend the day with me as a one-on-one client . . ."

Tony Robbins tells about a Back End client who pays him $1 million a year to meet with him once a month on the phone.

The big secret in life is that
there is no big secret. Whatever
your goal, you can get there
if you're willing to work.

- Oprah

SECTION 2:

YOUR PRODUCTS

& OFFERS

Chapter 8 – Buyer Psychology

The Secret of success is learning how to use pain and pleasure instead of having pain and pleasure use you. If you do that, you're in control of your life. If you don't, life controls you.
                                        - Anthony Robbins

Earlier we talked about knowing your market segments. We'll continue that process in this chapter and add to it talk about the psychology that moves individuals to buy. After all, your market is made up of individual who make decisions to buy or not buy from you. Even if your market is made up of big corporations, decision makers are individual people. (Refer back to this chapter often, people by with emotion, and this chapter gives good information to inform your marketing.

Win-Win Selling

The chances of selling are greatest when people want and need what we sell. The idea of "selling ice to the Eskimos" is no longer funny. First, the indigenous people of the North want to be called "Inuit." And people don't want to be sold stuff they don't need. Why should we even think of doing that's. Now, it's not "selling," it's "serving." It's guiding people to a decision - in the sales process - that is in their best interest. Period.

Stephen Covey, author of Seven Habits of Highly Effective People, said, "You should always seek a win-win, or say it's 'No deal!'" Consider this example. You've got a great best steak restaurant in town, serving only USDA Prime, with the best marbling and degree of maturity, with sides dripping in butter, and for desert, tiramisu, made with milk, heavy cream, and mascarpone cheese for desert.

But if the market is vegan, they don't care about what that you you're your steaks "best quality products." They don't care how delicious the cake is. They won't buy. Ever. They are actually offended by your offer. Don't be in the business of "selling ice to Eskimos," or "Inuit's."

Emotions that Affect Buyer Behavior

Dr. Peter Murray, in an article in *Psychology Today* magazine, entitled, "How Emotions Influence What People Buy," says there are many emotions involved in the buying process. As he says, "Consumers do not have a Pavlovian response to products and to their marketing programs. Nor do the fundamentals of consumer behaviors change to accommodate the latest innovation in digital technology." (Pavlov, a behavioral scientist, is known for training dogs to associate the ringing of a bell with getting food. The dogs started salivating with the ringing of a bell alone.)

An understanding of consumer purchase behavior must be based on knowledge of human emotion and include the paramount influence that emotions have on decision-making.

List of Buyers' Emotions

Business coach, consultant, and author of the "No BS" series, Dan S. Kennedy lists, in an article in Entrepreneur Magazine, the emotional drivers of buying behavior. "The fact is, everybody's buying behavior is driven by emotions, then justified as necessary, after the fact, with logic."

1. Greed. "If I make a decision now, I will be rewarded."

2. Fear. "If I don't make a decision now, I'm toast."

4. Envy. "If I don't make a decision now, my competition will win."

5. Pride. "If I make a decision now, I will look smart."

6. Guilt & Shame. "If I don't make a decision now, I will look stupid."

Notice that these emotions are all negative. Are people only motivated to buy to avoid pain? No, however . . . As Anthony Robbins
explains in his work, people are motivated by the threat of pain (and the avoidance of pain) and by pleasure. And people react more quickly to pain . . . and to avoid pain.

Maslow's Hierarchy of Needs

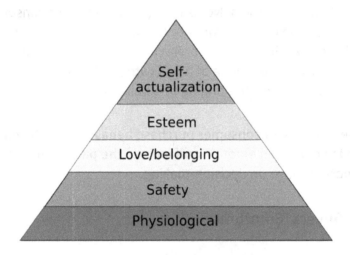

Maslow's Hierarchy of 5 Human Needs

1. Physiological

2. Safety

3. Love/Belonging

4. Esteem

5. Actualization

Now that we've listed what the Needs are, let's look at each of them individually.

1. **Physiological Needs** refer to the basic physical requirements for food, water, and shelter. If these needs are not met, or people are fearful about them being met, they will be insecure, distracted, an unavailable to seek the higher level needs.

   (As a side note, 12.7% of families in the United States suffered food insecurity in 2015, according to the United States Department of Agriculture. While they don't know where their next meal is coming from, these families are hardly in a position to be ambitious about creating successful, fulfilling lives.)

2. **Safety Needs** include personal security, as in freedom from harm; financial security, health and well being, and having a safety net (insurance) against accidents, illness and their adverse affects. Where there is insecurity because of war, natural disaster, family violence, childhood abuse, etc. – people may experience post-traumatic stress disorder or trauma.

   With less extreme insecurity, people still experience symptoms, which include stress, sleepless problems, and turning to food, alcohol or other substances to relieve the stress. Seeking relief from (or avoidance of) feeling lack of safety and security is a strong driver of behavior.

3. **Love & Belonging Needs,** according to Maslow, are strong motivators. People want to belong and be accepted in families, social groups, with co-workers, spiritual groups, professional organizations, and more. This need seeks friendships, intimacy, and family relationships. Without these, people can feel lonely, anxious, and even clinical depression.

   This need is strong. In the past, during tribal and communal times in history, threats of shunning were actually a death sentence. People depended on each other, not just for social reasons, but also for the safety that came from sharing resources and helping each other out.

Notice how the Needs overlap and have an affect on each other.

4. **Esteem Needs.** It's typical– and a driving force - for people to want to be accepted, admired, and valued by others. People often engage in a profession or hobby to gain recognition, to get awards, to "win" prizes and to receive other signs of their significance. These activities and awards give the person a sense of contribution or value.

   A desire for status is closely aligned to this Esteem Need. People dress, drive, and live in a way that communicates their status, so they can be esteemed by others, and feel special within themselves. Esteem Needs may include recognition, fame, prestige, attention, and feelings of significance.

   People respond well to VIP offers and products that set buyers apart from – and above – the rest.

   People not only want the respect and admiration of others, their self-esteem is also important. As Abraham Lincoln suggested, "When I do good, I feel good. When I do bad, I feel bad."
   Yet, sometimes people try to take a quicker path to feeling good by buying friendships and even the love of their children.

5. **Self-Actualization Needs.** This is characterized y the saying, "What a man can be, he must be." This need can be expressed in many ways. One individual may have the strong desire to become an ideal parent. In another, the

desire may be expressed athletically. For others, it may be expressed in paintings, pictures, or inventions.

These needs are strong drivers of behavior, motivation, and of buying decisions.
We can explain the housing bubble and economic crash in terms of Maslow's ideas on human needs.

Safety. In the US that American dream has long meant home ownership. Couple that deep need for security with the need for love and belonging and the scene is set. Dad and mom want to be good providers for their family. Suddenly it seems possible to have a dream house with all the trimmings, with a loan that required no qualifications.

While before, bread winners were satisfied to provide the basics, now it seemed they could use the equity in their homes as an ATM machine for home improvements, travel, and other luxuries.
Then, reality set in, the bubble popped. And it was time to "pay the Piper." There were a gazillion foreclosures.

On the banker's side, combinations of bad loans were packaged to provide seemingly safe investments. With all their degrees and experience that them to be cautious, they were caught with $dollar xxx problems.

While people were lead astray because of their inherent needs as Maslow defined them, and while they do want to buy more prudently, people still do buy for emotional reasons. They still buy from emotion then use logic to justify.

But they buy differently, with more of an expectation of value upfront.

We have talked here about emotions and needs that drive buyer behavior. How we convey those ideas to prospect and buyers is with images, ideas, layout, design, and words. Here are words that evoke emotion and add punch to your copywriting. The power words that follow, and writing, are important at several stages in the Sales Funnel. We'll talk about that later.

"Words have power" . . .
"Words begin and end wars.
They create and destroy families.
They break hearts.
They heal them.
If you have the right words,
there's nothin' on earth you can't do."

- Lori Handeland

List Of Power Words

1. **You** – Write as though you're speaking to the customer and about the customer, not about yourself.

2. **Because** – Give customers a reason why they need to take action.

3. **Free** – Because we all like free things, right?

4. **Value** – This implies customers are getting something versus losing something (i.e. money when you say "cost" or "price").

5. **Guaranteed** – Give customers a guarantee to minimize risk perception, so they feel they have everything to gain and nothing to lose.

6. **Amazing** – Customers will respond to something that is incredible.

7. **Easy** – Make it simple for customers to take the next step in the purchasing process, and let them know how much easier life will be with your product or service.

8. **Discover** – This implies there is something new and unknown to the customer, something that has supreme benefits and gives them an edge.

9. **Act now** – Motivate an immediate response with a limited-time offer.

10. **Everything included/everything you need** – This establishes that your product or service is all your customers will have to buy in order to achieve their goal.

11. **Never** – Point out a "negative benefit," such as "never worry again" or "never overpay again."

12. **New** – Your product or service is the cutting edge in your industry.

13. **Save** – The most powerful word to showcase monetary savings, or even time savings.

14. **Proven** – Remind customers that your product, service or business is tried-and-true.

15. **Safe and effective** – "Proven" to minimize risk perception for health and monetary loss.

16. **Powerful** – Let customers know that your business, product or service is robust.

17. **Real results/guaranteed results** – Your customers want results, after all.

18. **Secret** – Not everyone succeeds, and there are secrets to success. Let customers know you can reveal those secrets.

19. **The** – This implies your solution is the "end-all-be-all." Consider the difference: "3 Solutions for Marketing Success"/"The 3 Solutions for Marketing Success."

20. **Instant** –Instant access or downloads are more appealing than waiting.

21. **How to** – Start off with a solution so customers read the rest of your copy.

22. **Elite** –Your customers are among the best in the world. Invite newbies to join a highly desirable club.

23. **Premium** – Premium helps denote high quality.

24. **Caused by** – If your marketing literature builds a case for your product, transitional phrases such as "caused by," "therefore," and "thus" can help reinforce the logic of a purchase.

25. **More** – Do you offer more than your competitors? Let your customers know, because they want the best deal, after all.

26. **Bargain** – Because customers want a great deal, remember?

27. **No obligation** – Create a win-win situation for your customers.

28. **100% money-back guarantees** – Again, no risk.

29. **Huge** – A large discount or outstanding offer is difficult to resist.

30. **Wealth** – If you're selling products and services related to money, wealth is a desirable word for customers.

The Buying Trance

One of the reasons why 1st, 2nd and 3rd Up Sells work is because of the 'buying trance'. When a customer makes a purchase, they are in a mood to buy more. When someone has just bought, they are more inclined to make more purchase. By having multiple Up Sells, you are putting that emotional state to your advantage.

Good Return Policies Instill Confidence

There was a time when people would've made a long and serious consideration before making a purchase, especially on the Internet. But nowadays, people often purchase on a whim. This is because of the reliable refund policy that vendors have.

These refund policies are like a safety net and they are one of the big reasons why a customer feels safe making a purchase in the first place. If they're not happy with the product, they can just ask for their money back. The customer knows that they've got nothing to lose.

But, as a vendor, you want to avoid requests for refunds as best as you can. So, you need to offer nothing but the best products.

Now that we've talked about the psychology of selling and what motivates people, we'll start to look at the people in your market. The first step is to choose or define your market.

"The fact is, *everybody's* buying
behavior is driven by emotions,
then justified as necessary,
after the fact, with logic."

- - Dan Kennedy

Chapter 9 – Your Market & Opportunities

Before you can understand you market, you must learn more about the people and businesses included in it.

You can begin to learn more about your market with this three-step activity:

1. Create a list of people who would buy your product/service.

2. Break the list into categories.

3. Set priorities – which are the highest-probability buyers.

Consider this example: say you want to start a pest control company

1. Homeowners
2. Restaurants
3. Banks
4. Stadiums
5. Community centers
6. Buildings
7. Warehouses
8. Apartment owners
9. Theaters
10. Storage facilities
11. Funeral homes
12. Schools

1) Ask yourself:

- Of these types of buildings, which are most prone to problems with bugs?

- Which of these present the best marketing opportunities for you?

Given your answers, which of these prospects, which niche, might you want to focus on?

2) How to build categories?
Notice that prospects fall into three types:

1. Business to consumer (B to C)

2. Business to business (B to B)

3. Combination of the two (Combo)

There's a different sales process used for each niche. To use our pest control company example:

- **B to C** Includes homeowners & apartment owners

   We'd sell 1-on-1 selling to get individual orders

- **B to B** Is made up of commercial buildings

   We'd call managers/decision makers 1-on-1 & to get large

   orders. There may be a group approval process.

- **Combos** include property managers, real estate people who

   give referrals, and others

   We'd talk 1-on-1 to managers/decision makers of apartment

   complexes, homeowner's associations, and more

Choose which categories/niches to focus your business efforts on. In deciding, ask about: the size of the niche, and whether you have advantages and resources for reaching that niche. (We'll talk more about these later. As an example, a photographer can focus on:

1. Weddings, occasions

2. Portraits for families

3. Business headshots

4. Product shots

5. Real estate/architecture

6. Sports

7. Fashion

Notice that for each of these categories, the sales process, the gear required to perform, and the work itself is different.

The sports photographer must understand what kinds of shots clients will want and be prepared with the right gear to accommodate their desires. On the other hand, the fashion photographer will need a studio with the right lighting, an array of backgrounds, attire and props, a makeup artist, and models.

Let's look closer at a photographer as an example. It's easier for a photographer to get work when they have connections or can easily build connections. Ryan specializes in photographs for high-end real estate agents. He got his first job from a real estate agent in his community that he met at a charity fundraiser. He has gotten more work from people at church who are in the high-end real estate business. To get into high-end real estate photography he needed access to high-end people. That makes sense, doesn't it? (Later, we'll look at the connections you have.)

While we all need to prepare to reach large markets of people we don't know, when we are getting started, it's easier if we can "get a little help from our friends," with direct work or referrals.

Later, when we talk about your resources, we'll have you list who you know *and who knows you*, as well as other resources that make it easier for you to start and grow your business.

3) Create a profile of your niche, with their demographic details. Ask yourself these questions about your niche:

1. Where are they located, geographically?

2. What's their age range?

3. What's their gender?

4. Do they have children? If yes, what are their ages?

5. What's their education level?

6. What's their income level?

7. What's their marital or relationship status?

8. What is their work or profession?

9. What are their interests, what do they enjoy, and spend their time on?

10. What are their habits & behaviors, what do they do?

11. What are their values, what ideals do they hold dear?

Create a "Persona" of your niche.

To get clearer about your prospects and clients, create a profile (or persona) of one individual in your niche. Answer the above and add these questions:

1. What do they wear?

2. What do they drive?

3. What type of home do they live in?

4. Where do they hang out/shop online & social media?

5. Where do they hang out/shop in the offline world?

6. What events do they attend?

7. What do they do with their free time?

8. What interests are they active with?

9. What groups do they belong to?

10. What problems do they face?

11. What are their hopes and dreams?

12. Other _____

By answering questions from the two above lists, you build a composite, or persona, of someone in your niche. With the persona, the person can seem more real to you. You can put yourself in their shoes and get a better idea of what they need and want, what they will respond to, and what could cause them to move forward . . . or hesitate.

Get Targeted & Personal. When you create marketing and sales materials specifically designed for your niche, you will get better results. People say "Yes" more quickly when they feel you understand them and care about their results.

Here are a few more notes about choosing your niche:
First of all, choose a **large market**. For example, the health niches and personal development niches are very large. Both these markets are big enough to generate sales. There is completion in large niches – lots of it. But as you offer your message in your unique style, your approach h – they will buy from you.

Your **research is crucial**, because in different niche, you'll meet different kind of customers with different mindsets. Once you can put yourself in your ideal customers' shoes, attracting traffics to your site, getting them to sign up for your emails, getting the ball rolling with your Front End product, and then generating big sales is assured.

Once you identify the market, **consider what kind of Lead Magnet** that will attract them **and a Front End pro**duct that you can sell to them. When you are able to target them, your Front End offer is going to lead you to massive sales.

3) Set Priorities - Example
One of the most admired and biggest-earning human performance trainers of our time is Anthony Robbins. When he was getting started there were two bold moves he made to make a name for himself and

to attract business. First, he toured Canada and invited therapists to

"bring me your toughest patients. I'll help them (live, on TV) cure their phobia in five minutes." Next, he produced events in the backyard of his castle (yes, he literally lived in a castle) in Del Mar, where he led people in the Fire Walk Experience.

Let's make a guess at the Sales Funnel that got Tony Robbins started on his path to fame and fortune.

1) 1st LEAD MAGNET - TV tour around Canada –This was a great Lead Magnet – the TV station fielded calls for him. People got to see him for free on TV. Before the Internet, this was a great way to go . . . it still is.

2) PRODUCT - Fire Walk – At his castle in Del Mar, CA, he set up a fire walk in his back yard, and the rest is history. (This wasn't a free event, so it wasn't a Lead Magnet. It was an Up Sell.)

3) FRONT END PRODUCT – Book

4) UP SELL PRODUCT - Live Classes & workshops

5) UP SELL PRODUCT – Video programs (originally sold on infomercials, not sold online)

6) BACK END – Certification programs (original back end)

7) BACK END – Speaker, Big, Big Bucks

8) BACK END - Now, he takes contracts for one-on-one sessions that are Big, Big Bucks, with presidents, sports stars, financial market stars, and others who want his services and can afford the price.

I don't share Tony's story to intimidate you, but to impress upon you that with little cash, loads of passion and charisma, and the right product – you too can build your business into a moneymaking machine.

When it comes to building his business, Robbins was very bold. From claiming that he could turn around any phobia in minutes – live on TV – to a Fire Walk Experience, he's a great role model, don't you think?

People want their needs met, they also want storytelling, entertainment, and education.

"It's time for a little pep talk.
Stop being boring. Yes I mean you. "
- Kid President

Chapter 10 – Your Products

We've talked about your market and created a persona, now we'll talk about you, your resources, and your opportunities. From that, you'll become clearer about what products will work best for you.

In this chapter we'll begin to look at how to develop your products.

Some ideas are useful for all the products you create. So, we'll share them in this chapter, which you can refer to when you begin creating the different types of products: Lead Magnet, Up Front, Up Sell, Cross Sell, Down Sell, and Back End.

You should also refer to the other chapters to remind yourself of the other elements that go into your products: emotion, needs, power words, and more. For now, though, let's talk about your interests. **About You and Your Brand.** Who are you?

1. Spiritual, know yourself
2. Health & fitness
3. Growth & learning
4. Family, friends, Social
5. Money & finance
6. Career & business
7. Relationship status
8. Community
9. Time of life
10. Fun
11. Home & environment
12. What are your values
13. What drives you
14. What's important to you

What resources do you already have that you need for building your product? Fill out the chart below as an inventory of the skills and resources you have now. Then, think of when you used those skills.

- Maybe it was in school, even in elementary school.

- Maybe it was when you were in a club or group activity and you pitched in.
- Maybe it's been a casual interest, but you were good at it or had it in you to do it.

(We're talking here about your products, but while you're making this assessment, you might as well consider other business opportunities and possibilities.)

In looking at your resources, think of your products and your business as mountain climbing. You can't just get it in your head to climb x mountain. You need to train to get in shape for the challenge, learn how to use the gear, to deal with possible situations, to navigate, and more. You need to have the gear, a guide, and others to take the trip with you.

It's the same with building your products and your business. You must assess what you need, what you've got and make the most of what you've got, in order to reach your destination.

"Our research has found that people are usually willing to pay more to get a better consumer experience."

- Tony Bodoh

Item	Details	How to use this
Skills		
Writing		
Speaking		
Photos		
Video		
Humor		
Storytelling		
Organizing		
Analyzing		
Managing		
Leadership		
Enrolling/Engaging		
Other		
Gear/Equipment		
Computer		
Software, Applications		
Smart Phone		
Other		
Materials		
Ingredients		
Tools		
Other		
Assets		
Artwork/Illustrations		
Photos		
Videos		
Power Point/Keynote		
Writings		
Other		
Spending/Budget		
Earnings		
Cash		
Barter		
Other People's		
Joint Venture		
Other		
Marketing & Promos		
Social Media		
Affiliates		
Joint Ventures		
Advertising		
Time		
Yours		
Others		

You don't have to start your products from nothing; you already have skills and resources. Take stock of your interests, characteristics, and resources – then let that information inspire your product ideas.

There's one more important resource, your connections. Often your connections can help you get a leg up on starting to sell your products or growing your business. Because of that, it makes sense to look at your connections before you begin to build your products.

Earnings		
Cash		
Barter		
Other People's		
Joint Venture		
Other		
Marketing & Promos		
Social Media		
Affiliates		
Joint Ventures		
Advertising		
Time		
Yours		
Others		

It's great if you already have connections. Most people don't have as many as they would like. The good news is, you can build your connections.

How To Build Your Connections

David Israel started his company, Pop Gourmet! – And within four years was offering his unique snack foods all over the country, at Starbucks, Bed Bath & Beyond, and many more stores. Early on he got into Oprah's magazine as one of her favorite things.

Israel had two big hooks that seemed to interest Oprah. First, his popcorn is amazing, with toppings that make you swoon with delight. And, over 30% of his employees were formerly incarcerated, who happen to be African Americans. Oprah has a heart for people who help down and out communities – and that would be David Israel. Israel gives people a chance at a job and a life, when others turn their backs on them.

What Products Are Best For You?

Now that you are more aware of your resources and connections, now we are more ready to start looking at what products are best for you to create. Well, almost. There are a few more ideas we'll look at first.

Knowing that you can build more connections, consider who can be helpful, and in what ways they can help. Israel sought Oprah out, as well as other publicity, and that was very helpful in getting investors, getting distribution, and more.

What can you do to increase your connections and influence?
Follow Your Passion?

We hear a lot of talk about "doing what you love and the money will follow." I asked Taylor Banks, ecommerce Expert, his thoughts on this subject.

He was very clear, "It's nice to choose a product that you are passionate about. But what's more important is offering products that *others* are passionate about. If there are many people who are Interested in a topic and product, you'll make lots of sales. If others are *not* so interested in what you're interested in, you won't do well."

That makes perfect sense, doesn't it?

Cindy is in school and thinking about creating a side-hustle business. Cindy likes to draw whimsical figures and is pretty good at it. She is good at researching on the Internet and found a gal who draws characters for little kids. The characters are running, dancing, doing yoga, eating, reading, and all kinds of activities.

Known simply as "Margaret" on Etsy, she is one of their top sellers with her "Once More With Love Munchkin" stickers. Margaret has racked up over 200,000 in orders in since 2015. She prints her characters on stickers and sells them in sheets. At $4 a sheet, not too bad, huh? That's $800,000
Margaret has one Up Sell product – character stickers. As popular as they are, she could make more money, and spread around more smiles if she expanded her product line.

More Creativity Than Cash
Superhero Reality TV on YouTube is a very low-cost big-income-earning business. While their business doesn't rely on a successful Sales Funnel, it is a great example of using "more creativity than cash."

Watch their channel. Many of the videos have over 10,000,000 views. Notice what they have invested in, to generate those millions of views – and a great income:

- Stories

- "Actors"

- Home as backdrop

- Purchased costumes

- Music (may be public domain)

- Friends as actors

A YouTube channel like this, which regularly gets 7 million or 10 million hits per video, can earn $50,000 a month.

More Hustle Than Cash

For our documentary movie, The Elephant in Your Room, we interviewed Brian Hamilton, from "Inmates to Entrepreneurs." Their program is exactly as it sounds; they teach inmates how to build businesses. One of their graduates had just $25 when he got out of prison. He started a painting business, grew it over time, and sold it for $3 million. Now he does business consulting and real estate investing.

I've been so inspired by Hamilton's work that we're developing programs for how to start service businesses, maid service, catering, and other businesses.

These service businesses are great for inmates because they require very little in the way of resources. However, they do require hands-on labor and hustle. I figure they are also excellent business types for other people. And, according to SCORE, they can have an 80% success rate.

You don't have to be passionate about the work you do, but you do have to be passionate about serving others with your products – enough to do what it takes and to continue when the going gets rough. It also helps to be passionate about reaching your goals, building a life of financial freedom, and living the life you envision for yourself and your family.

Price To Sell

There's lots said about how to price your products. We've talked a lot about your market, as well as your resources. When it comes to sell your products – including your Lead Magnet and Front End products – your resources and connections can make a big difference in what products you should build and how you should price them.

Obviously, your budget can make a difference in how you sell.

The quickest route to building your list and getting your Sales Funnel going is with paid advertising. Plus you need to have your products and you can spend a lot to produce them.
There's another element to look at, in terms of how you sell – and that will have a lot to do with how you should price your products.

You can pay for advertising.

Or you can pay affiliates.

An affiliate will promote your Front End product to their list. Why? They've got customers who buy stuff. If there is a match between your affiliate and your products, it's a match made in marketing heaven! Why do they promote your products to their list? So the can make more money from their list!

They will not promote a free Lead Magnet; they can't make a commission off of a free product! But they'll be happy to promote your Front End, if you have all your marketing elements in place.

Now, there's a lot to be said for Internet Front End products to be priced at $7 to $27 because that's a comfortable price for buyers who don't yet know you. However, even if you give 100% commission of a $7 to $27 product, that's not an exciting income opportunity for the affiliate.

But, if you create a Front End product that gives big value and can be sold for $100, now you can go one of two ways.

- You can give the affiliate 50%, so they get $50. Not bad.

- Or you can pay 70% commission and they get, well, $70.

- Or you can pay 100% so they get $100.

Knowing that these promotional methods are available, when it comes to building your products, you can follow Stephen Covey's advice and "begin with the end in mind."
If you want affiliates to be excited about offering your product, you should plan to make a really high-value offer, something priced at $100, something that people would say they got $1,000 worth of value from, something that will make the affiliate and the buyer happy.

To sell a $100 product with no Lead Magnet takes some doing. You need social proof: publicity, testimonials, samples, or other evidence that your stuff is great, so people feel confident shelling out $100. Of course, a money back guarantee helps the buyer, but the affiliate doesn't want any charge backs! They want to be sure that the money that comes in from them promoting you to their list will stay in their pockets.

If you're going with another approach, selling on social media and from your website (with or without advertising), you may want to go with the free Lead Magnet, $7 to $27 Front End product, and $100 to $250 Up Sell and then take it from there. You can add unlimited Up Sells. As long as you have more value to share, you can keep Up Selling. And of course there are the Back End products, too.

Now, we talked about affiliates selling your stuff to their list. As you build your list, you will be able to sell other people's stuff and you make the 100% commissions. Selling other people's products can become a part of you Sales Funnel.

Amy Porterfield Story
Porterfield created content first as part of Harley Davidson's internal marketing team, and then for performance coach Tony Robbins. From live events to podcasts to product launches, Porterfield has done it all, and done it well. When Porterfield went out on her own, she got affiliates to promote her $100 product for her.

Affiliate sales worked for Porterfield and it can work for you. Note: beware of companies that offer a "work at home, laptop lifestyle business" where you are supposed to sell their products - after you have paid a hefty fee for the privilege of doing so. It's already going to cost you to sell other's products. It cost you to build your list, or if you advertise their products, there's a definite cost.

There should be no fee involved to be an affiliate. Period. I know of one company that calls what is essentially an affiliate program a "licensing program." Beware of that kind of offer. One such company actually teaches attendees at their $250 program how to increase their credit limit, and encourages them to do so at the lunch break. Why? So they can go into debt to get the money to buy a license – for thousands to tens of thousands of dollars. Did I say beware?

Set Yourself Up For Success
Before we start building your products, there's one more piece of information you need.

On the next page, look at the top reason businesses fail: Mostly because the product is not what the market needs or wants. This chart, from CB Insights shows the reasons startups fail. As we've said before, Find what your market wants and give them that.

The core products of your business – and your Lead Magnet and Front End products - are key to your success.

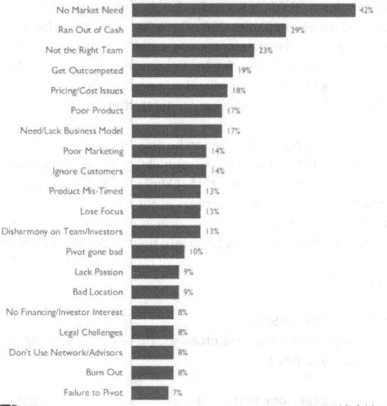

Top 20 Reasons Startups Fail
Based on an Analysis of 101 Startup Post-Mortems

Reason	Percentage
No Market Need	42%
Ran Out of Cash	29%
Not the Right Team	23%
Get Outcompeted	19%
Pricing/Cost Issues	18%
Poor Product	17%
Need/Lack Business Model	17%
Poor Marketing	14%
Ignore Customers	14%
Product Mis-Timed	13%
Lose Focus	13%
Disharmony on Team/Investors	13%
Pivot gone bad	10%
Lack Passion	9%
Bad Location	9%
No Financing/Investor Interest	8%
Legal Challenges	8%
Don't Use Network/Advisors	8%
Burn Out	8%
Failure to Pivot	7%

CB INSIGHTS   www.cbinsights.com

Chapter 11 - Produce Your Products

Following are ideas about producing a couple kinds of products.

Remember, "Begin with the end in mind." Keep your market, your resources, and how you will get in front of people in mind. Also take into consideration how your Sales Funnel can work with Up Sells, Cross Sells, Down Sells, and Back End products to create top ROI income and give customers more of what they want.

Consider which methods you will use to get your products in front of your market. Your marketing plans make a difference in the products you develop.

- Use Affiliates – they promote you

- Use webinars – you promote, or affiliates promote

- Use Social Media – you promote, affiliates promote

- Use paid ads – Google, FaceBook, or other

- Use presentations & events – you host, or others do

- Get meaningful exposure – others promote you

- Build your authority – write your book, get awards, etc.

- Build your connections – you develop these

- Set your payment plan - to fit your resources

Be Encouraged

Know that you're taking the right steps. Be patient. Stay the course.

- If you need accountability to stay on track, you might consider hiring a success coach. (We're building a cost-effective Membership specifically to fulfill these needs for coaching, networking, success celebrations, and more.)

- If you crave brainstorming and encouragement, join a mastermind group, associations, or groups that will give you what you need.

We've already stated the importance of understanding your market and what they need and want. Refer back to all the information presented in this book. With that information you are ready to create products.

Here are four ways you can get your Lead Magnet and Front End products done:

1. Create them by yourself – We offer DIY programs. Obviously this takes more of your time, but less money.
2. Get help producing them – We held with Done For You service.
   Use a ghostwriter, a coach, or a full Done For You Service. (Print on Demand is okay for books; you don't need to make money with these offerings, anyhow.)
3. Use a combination of using your own work and getting guidance/help from others – Our DIY and DFY can help
4. Offer someone else's product

We'll talk mostly about creating product yourself and focus on the How To's for creating a book and a video program.

Please realize that this is not a comprehensive description of how to create your products. Product is just one part of the Sales Funnel. It is an important part, but there's not room here to share all the information you will need. **(Check our other programs, Done For You Services, or for more help with creating products.)**

If someone else is creating your products, they will give you the process you need to follow to work with them. Also, offering someone else's product is another broad topic; we won't cover that here. We will touch on that subject later.

Why You Need Your Book

Mike Schultz, principal of the Wellesley Hills Group, decided to find out why – or whether – business people should write books and surveyed 200 business-book authors. In an article in BusinessWeek, Schulz said "The vast majority of the authors we surveyed -- 96% -- said they did realize a significant positive impact on their businesses from writing a book and would recommend the practice." 96%!

Your book will be great for:

- Building your reputation.

- Increasing your credibility in the marketplace,

- Your products will make more sales.

- Earning higher fees from speaking, consulting, or other offers.

- Grabbing the attention of industry leaders.

- Attracting help from industry leaders and others.

- Your ticket to get publicity with TV, radio, magazines, and blogs.

- The perception that yours is "the" brand to buy.

Print Or Print On Demand?

When It comes to producing your book, you will decide to go "Print on Demand" (where your upfront cost is very low but you make very little per book) or go with a publisher (which means you'll have to pay up front for printing many copies of your books). There are pluses and minuses with both methods.

Book, eBook, or Both?

Again, whether you choose to do a physical book or eBook should depend on what you want to accomplish, your resources, and how you will market & use your books. I go to conferences and will be doing appearances on TV and radio, so it's best for me to have physical books to offer.

There is more involved in a physical book; it has to be formatted for printing, which is a different set up than the format for an eBook. That adds another pesky task to your To Do List. But, the impression a physical book makes – and the doors it can open – are way greater than what an eBook can accomplish.
You may want to have both kinds of books available – a physical book and an eBook.

An eBook is quicker and more cost effective to produce. EBooks are actually preferred by most readers now. Plus having your eBook posted on Amazon.com is great for SEO (search engine optimization). When someone searches for your name, your Amazon posting will show. Nice.

An Audio Book is another option you should consider for your book. Many people (including me) would rather listen to a book than to read it. I love being able to learn while I drive, exercise, or during other activities; others do to.

Create it Yourself

First, brainstorm ideas and decide on the topic for your book and other products. When it comes to your Front End product, you already know how important it is to pick the right topic, because if the Front End doesn't make the first sale and open the buying loop, the whole sales funnel – and your profit potential - will flop. The Up Sell products are where you make your money, so they are important to.

Once you've decided on what topic you are going to use for your Front End, you need to ask yourself a question: "How are you going to teach people?"

- Is it going to be from your own experience?
- Is it going to be from what your research?
- Will you interview people?
- Will you use a combination of the above?

Three Ways to "Write" Your Book

- Sit down and start writing.
- Make an audio recording of your content and have it transcribed, edited, and formatted.
- Hire someone else as a ghostwriter to create your product.

About Writing Your Book

1) The most important step before you start writing is to make an outline. This narrows the focus of your research and your content.

2) List the sub-points for under each chapter.

3) List chapters one-by-one, and then put them in order to have the general overview of your book.

4) This process will ensure that the flow of the whole content is smooth and that, when you are researching you don't get lost finding material you don't need for your book. In the beginning, don't worry too much about the sequence. The sequence of the chapters can always change afterwards.

Then, you can start writing the content.

The most important thing for you to know is that writing a book is simpler than you think. Like anything worthwhile, it takes time and self-disciple, but you *can* do it! It's simple, but not necessarily easy.

It's like Ernest Hemingway said, "There's nothing to writing. All you do is sit down and open a vein."

Having said that, I'm reminded of one of my favorite sayings, from the movie, "A League of Their Own," "It's supposed to be hard. If it were easy everyone would do it."

The thing is: it's easy "enough." After all, you know the subject, and you are highly motivated – remember, 96% of authors benefit in a very big way. Soon that'll be you!

To write and complete your book, you need good organization, planning, writing, and revisions.

It will take time to write your book. Probably more than you think. You can either "just do it," and the time it takes to write it, at once. Or plan to do your writing over time. Scheduling time works well. Like anything else, put writing time in your schedule. Then, like Nike says, "Just do it!"

(I'm a "get 'er done" kinda gal. But do what works best for you.)

If you write the book over time it's extremely important for you to stick with it until it's finished. Set a plan to work a certain number of hours each week and schedule your writing time in your calendar. For designing you cover and back cover, as well as other graphic elements of your book and other products, consider using Fiverr.

Unless you are good at creating graphics and layouts, a Fiverr expert will be able to do the work for you quickly, easily and cost effectively.

Do Your Book First, Before Creating Other Products

It will take more time to complete a book compared to creating video training courses, webinars or other products. However, if you get the book done first, the hard, lengthy part is out of the way - and you'll have the already have gathered the materials you need as the foundation for your other products.

Plus, having a book makes a great impression, builds your credibility and authority, separates you from those who haven't paid the price by writing a book, and gives TV, radio and online media reasons to interview and promote you. It's the best calling card.

With all these benefits, it's easy to get motivated and to get your book done.

You can use the first twenty pages of your book, along with the cover, as a Lead Magnet. In my case, there are graphics we created for the book that are great Lead Magnets. We also use those graphics as handouts at events and in our other marketing.

You can also use a PDF of the book as a free gift for your top customers, supporters, and joint venture partners.

You don't even have to have the book completed before you offer PDF copies of book samples as your Lead Magnet. In addition, I've often created the book cover, gotten it printed, and wrapped it around another book, so I can have a picture of myself and the book *before* the book is even printed (or completed, for that matter).

Know this about your book: You probably won't make money from it. But, you will increase your "business celebrity," and gain entrée to high-end contacts and publicity. You send printed copies of your book to TV and radio show producers, as well as bloggers who can give you massive exposure. More doors will open for you. What you do with those opportunities – and your Sales Funnel - will determine what the ROI from your book is.

You will be able to use your book as a Lead Magnet to attract sponsors, investors, for TV and radio producers, and joint venture opportunities. That's where your book will make you money - as your "calling card" and door opener.

Your Video & Transcripts and/or Workbook Product

If you've already written your book, many of the steps required for your video program are already completed. (This is different than a promotional or explainer video. This video is actual product.) If you are starting with your video program, it's the same process as for writing your book: brainstorm ideas, outline, collect materials, and then write your content.

Hard Copy or Digital? Plus Pricing

People will pay $150 for some video programs and $1,500 (or much more) for others. The difference is often about the marketing and already-perceived authority and "celebrity" of the producer/author.

What It Takes to Get Paid Well

Be realistic in planning what to charge – and what people will actually pay.

> "We don't get paid what we 'deserve;'
>
> we get what we 'earn.'"
>
> - Anonymous

Part of how we earn higher prices is by doing the work of marketing, as well as establishing your authority and social proof.

As an example, let's say that you have plenty of funds for your Sales Funnel project, including creating all the social proof you need, with advertising, publicity, posting content, and engaging on social media – you will be able to command whatever price you want for your product, within reason.

You set the odds in your favor of getting top dollar for your program if you make the program a hard copy – with a workbook, DVDs and other printed materials. With the design, graphics, and production, a hard product can require substantial up-front costs. But the actual production cost per unit can be as little as $50. Then there's packing, warehousing, and handling, for another $30. If you are getting paid $1,500, that's not a bad ROI – You spend $80 to earn $1,420.

On the other hand, if you are short on funds, you won't be able to pay to *quickly* get all the social proof you need to get higher prices. Further, creating hard products is pricey, with graphic design, layout, and more. It's way more costly than the price of your book. Then, to get a decent price on producing your program, you'll need to order many – hundreds, maybe many hundreds. So, there are big up-front costs.

In the end, the $80 cost out of the $150 you can get paid is, well, that's not exciting. In fact with your marketing and other costs, you may end up making very little. That's not how to become successful!

But, if you offer everything in a digital format, your Up Front product per copy cost go to almost nothing. That said, you still should create graphic images of your "products" to post online. Plus, all other elements - from the page layout, music, voice over, power point slides, and other elements of your digital product - should be top notch.

Affiliates

With your Up Sell products, realize that you can *still* have affiliates promote them for you. In fact your higher priced products will be more attractive to them. The more you can help your affiliates earn, the better results you'll receive from their promotions.

Creating Your Presentation Slides

The first step in creating your video program is to create presentation slides for each module with PowerPoint or Keynote. I love creating slides, they help streamline my writing, organize the main points, and make the material clear, concise, and sharp.

Create a script to use while you create the presentation. If you're like me, you will say things differently while you are creating the slides. Make changes to your script along the way. Doing it this way, when you're done with the slides, you'll have the audio script – and transcripts – completed.

Some people prefer to create the slides and then write the script. There is no "right" way; do what works best for you.

The Transcript Has 2 Purposes:
1. It is read for the audio recording by yourself or voiceover actor.
2. It is the written transcript you offer with the video training course.

Guidelines for Presentation Slides
1. Do not fill 100% of your slides with words. Less is more.
2. Put only the important points in the slides
3. You can have just 2 or 3 points in a slide
4. Present the full text of material in your audio track and/or transcripts.
5. Watch TedTalks presentations for ideas on how to use text and images in your slide presentations. (Of course TedTalks are a different format because the speakers are with the audience, but you'll still get ideas you can use, anyhow.)

About Your Voice Over

It's most cost effective to do your own audio track. But, be realistic, do you sound good enough on your recording? If not, consider asking someone on your team who does sound good to do the recording. That said, your audience will probably prefer to hear your message from you. So, make it a part of your professional development path to become a good enough speaker. Toastmasters International is one of the best – and most cost-effective - resources for improving your speaking.

To create your voiceover, you will read the script, but you shouldn't sound like you're reading. Read it aloud first (maybe several times) so you can read smoothly without stumbling over words or phrases. People often think that if they make a mistake it can be fixed with editing. This is true, but it's *much* better to get it right while you're recording.

Perfect Practice Makes Perfect

If you're new to sound recording, do a test recording of yourself before you do your voice over recording. Check for any problems in your speaking and work to be better. I tend to be a slow talker; I have to make a conscious effort to speak more quickly when I'm recording.

Make certain that you are getting good sound. I use a Blue Snowball microphone and record with Garage Band on my Mac. The quality of recording on your smart phone may be good enough – if you use a plug-in mic – and if the phone is new enough to produce high quality. Check it out before you plan on recording – or anywhere. Sound quality is crucial to the impression your product makes.

Make it Easier on Yourself

Plan to record short segments. Unless you are practiced at doing voiceovers, don't plan on doing 20 or 30 or 90 minutes at a time. It's easy to edit short clips together with your slides and/or video. If you are recording during a live session, your audience will be more forgiving, but not much. I said it before, I'll say it again – good sound is mega important. People do not want to strain to hear your message.

When you have you Power Point presentation and your voiceover done, you edit them together. I use iMovie on my Mac. If you are a PC person, use their video-editing software.

For a really professional look, create an "intro" and "outro" for your video, with your branding. These are best when done with AfterEffects software. Or consider having someone from Fiverr create these for you. They will be under 10 seconds long each, so it's a small, inexpensive job for them to do.

Your Transcript

You may want to add the transcript to your video product offer. This provides more value for your customer. They scroll through the transcript to get to the points they want to review. Or if your product is delivered digitally, they can print the transcript out and flip through it.

Better Yet, Add a Workbook

To increase the perceived and actual value of your product, add a workbook to go along with the Video program.

To create your workbook, use your presentation slides, add questions and blanks to fill in. Give examples in the workbook (from the book)

And you're about done. To create a much better perception of value, design it. Add formatting, graphics and images. Format the pages so they look nice, maybe use a border around the page, or a branded header at the top and your copyright and contact information on the bottom.

Make it Easier on Yourself, Again
If you are not a whiz at layout and design, that's understandable. So, there's a quicker, easier way than doing that work in your desktop publishing program, like MS Word, or whatever you use. Use PowerPoint or Keynote. You got that right. The slides become the pages in your workbook, so they will be landscape orientation, but that adds to the stylized look of your finished product.

Choose a PowerPoint template that fits with your branding, build your workbook pages just like you did with your presentation - Easy, peasy. Doing it this way, your workbook will look awesome – and so will you.

Can you turn your Power Point-produced into a PDF? Yep. Not only that, you can burn it as a DVD, or turn it into a movie to upload on YouTube. Just load it as "private" and give your customers the code to download it.

Even if you deliver your program online, suggest that people print it out and put it into a binder. This is a great resource, helping them really "work" with the information you present. And their binder remains on their shelf, as a reminder of you and your work – and how you helped them.

Other Product Options
Consider what you've got, in terms of products and resources. Review the information you gathered earlier about your skills, resources, and connections. Then put on your thinking cap to come up with Lead Magnets, Front End, and other Up Sell products.

As I'm writing, this just came across my computer:

That is a nice Front End product, isn't it? Or it's a nice Up Sell (or Down Sell) for an existing customer.

Think of how the Waldorf could make the offer even sweeter by bundling their free night with a deal from a nearby restaurant, Broadway show, limousine service, or airline tickets.
As you start thinking in terms of your Sales Funnel and offering more value and products to your customers, your creative juices can really start flowing.

When you are open to including other vendors in your offers, there are many advantages. Customers love the additional options. Your "partners" promote themselves and you to their lists.

"Deep within your mind lies a reservoir
of untapped genius and power.
Now is your time to release it."

- John Assaraf

Chapter 12 - Your Irresistible Lead Magnet

In a chapter about being irresistible, we must take a moment to remember Robert Palmer and the beautiful porcelain skinned, red-lipped, black-dress wearing, guitar-playing women, singing the lyrics, "You used to be good to me but now you are . . . Simply Irresistible." Words for you to live by: Don't just be good, be "simply irresistible"!

For me, the definition of the word "Irresistible" includes a reference to chocolate. So, the queen of the Lead Magnet has got to be Mrs. Fields, with her chocolate chip cookies.
When Debbie opened her first shop, frustrated and afraid to fail, she took samples of her cookies to people on the streets. They loved the samples and returned to actually buy cookies.

Providing free samples to potential customers remained a cornerstone of her business in the years to come.

Cinnabon is another example of an irresistible Lead Magnet. Only for them, they lure people into their shop by pumping out the fragrance of their buns. Be creative in your thinking about what will attract your market.

If your product is great, give away samples to attract customers – samples are a great Lead Magnet
Other stores let customers sample their wares, too. At the Microsoft store, you can try out their virtual reality product. It's fun for the person trying it out and fun for others to watch, too.

Eric Ludt is one of the "Cheese Brothers" at Mall of America in Minneapolis. Ludt has a great lead magnet; try his cheese samples and you will be walking out with cheese. Period. Sampling has worked so well for him, he made a profit from day one, even with the mega-expensive rents at Mall of America.

- What kinds of Lead Magnets have worked on you in brick and mortar stores - to get your foot into the door of their store, to get you to sample their wares?
- How about online?
- Did you buy after sampling?
- What other Lead Magnets have you said "Yes" to?

Make your Irresistible offer fun, cool, helpful, or all of the above. One way or another, make it valuable. The point is to give people an experience, with a Wow factor, that gives them an idea about your product and you, as your brand's ambassador.

2 Types Of Lead Magnets: PR & Samples

PR-Type Lead Magnet
You can build these Lead Magnets around holidays or other already-planned events. Or you can make up your own attention-getting ideas that will work anytime.

As an example, when Halloween is coming up, Can you have people buy their pumpkins from you and then have an onsite pumpkin-carving contest? Or even if you don't sell pumpkins, can you provide the pumpkins and then you have a carving contest – off line. Or can you have a pumpkin carving contest where people upload online pics of their jack-o-lanterns for others to vote on? Of course you can. These are fun, engaging, and may even get you local TV or radio publicity. You can certainly get Social Media attention from this.

PR-Type Lead Magnet Idea
At Mall of America, at the Tesla store, I saw men taking pictures of their gals in the red hot Tesla on display there. Well, as a filmmaker, I like to think I have an eye for images. So I offered to pose women so their guys could take their pictures in the car. Picture long legs in sexy shoes stepping out of the car. I had the women sit way back so you couldn't see them, just their legs. One woman went and bought new shoes for her photo opp. We were all having so much fun. It was a party!

While two or three sales people stood by, I thrilled the people in the store. Tesla's crew could have taken the pics –I'm sure each person in the store talked about the photos and the pics I took were sent all over the Internet.

This Lead Magnet took zero cash, zero equipment except a smart phone. I call it "More creativity than cash." What does it cost to turn a day at the mall into a fun, memorable, share-worthy event? A little creativity and $0! "There's always a budget for FREE!"

Sample-Type Lead Magnet

Use this list to prompt your thinking on what you can develop as a lead magnet.
- Guide, report
- Cheat sheet

- Resource list
- Info-graphic
- Assessment or Test
- Interview for publication
- Coupon Discount

- Photo or Video Opportunities
- Best Chapter of eBook
- Video training
- Free trial
- Other

After having seen the PR example and the Sample list – and considering your resources – and the fact that you will make no money from your Lead

Magnet – What Can Your Lead Magnet Be?

- What will give people so much value that they'll be happy to trade you for the email address?
- What will Wow people enough that they become open to your other offers?
- What will thrill people so they'll want to tell a friend

Now, you may not be able to give an exact sample of your product, but you can give a sample of how you and your company operate, what your values are, and more. And there's the PR-type Lead Magnet for that.

The problem with not having your own Lead Magnet is, once they have received their gift, they must be impressed enough with you that they continue to receive and read your emails. You don't want to spend $5 on a gift card to get a lead in your email list and then have them immediately unsubscribe.

Your Lead Magnet is closely related to your products and/or your brand. For example, for a company that helps alleviate stress, a Lead Magnet could be a video that helps create relaxation with positive affirmations and soft music. That's better than a coffee gift card because the company doesn't sell coffee. Of course, a free cup of coffee is a great Lead Magnet for a coffee shop! Or, as an incentive to meet face to face.

These options are not ideal because of the cost. However, to get people into your Sales Funnel, you will need an incentive.

What Can You Use As Your Lead Magnet?

Later will talk in more depth about some types of products, and samples of which can be Lead Magnets. As I'm writing this book, which can be a Front End or Cross Sell product, it occurs to me that I could give the first two chapters of this book as a Lead Magnet. When you have a book, you can do the same. However, I think some of the graphics I've created for the book, along with a one-page cheat sheet may work even better.

Should You Use a Freebie Of Other's Products?
Some people use others' products as a Lead Magnet. They'll give a Starbucks card, or some other incentive to get email subscribers.

Consider this, though. When someone trades their email for a cup of coffee, what they're saying is that they'd like a free cup of coffee. They may feel some good will toward you and may feel it's a nice gift, so you build good will. But they will *not* have said that they are interested in your brand or your product. So when they start getting emails from you on a subject they may have little or no interest in, they may unsubscribe. They may even forget that they signed up with you and report your emails as Spam. Yikes. So . . .

Much better to use a Lead Magnet that is related to you and your product by using the PR-type product or, better yet, a sample of your product.

The Good News Is:
With your freebie product, people don't expect – or even want - big comprehensive products! It's often best for your offer to be four pages or less.

Think of Mrs. Fields, she didn't give a whole cookie, and she certainly didn't give a box of cookies. It's the same with your samples; it's a "taste" of good things to come, not the whole product. And, it does satisfy one problem for your new subscriber.

Always Be Serving

Prospects trade their emails to get the value they want . . . they are happy with that. Then they become more interested in making an actual investment. Once they learn that you do give great value, now they are more open to what else you offer.

Not to throw in an ad here, but okay, I just have to. In our Sales Funnel Workshop, we help people actually decide on what products will be best for them and begin building them.

Notice how natural it is for me to share that. I'd even be remiss if I didn't let you know that we have that next-level product available. Notice, don't you feel "served" instead of "sold"? Since it's something you may feel a need for, the approach feels natural, comfortable, and welcomed (not pushy or sales-y).

Remember, what we said earlier about the Customer Lifetime Value. That figure you came up with is what the value of the Lead Magnet is to you. Your Lead Magnet is an investment in future business.

There's No "Right" Way

Sometimes the Lead Magnet – goes right into the up sell:

- At the toy store kids play and parents buy. There's no need for a first step, Front End product.

- Time Share – lead magnet, discounted tickets to amusement park, trips, or even cash. No Front End product
- Neil Patel – has no Front End product. He goes from Lead Magnet to Up Sell.

How to Put Your Lead Magnet to Work

If you have a store-front business, obviously, you sample at your location.

But, you gather emails to keep in touch with people. Even for brick-and-mortar businesses, email follow-up and promotions can generate a lot of sales. So whether for an offline or online business, these are important:

- **Website.** When it comes to Internet marketing, your website is where much of the action of your Sales Funnel springs from, and returns to.
- **Landing Page.** Lead Generation usually happens on a Landing Page (which can be on your website).
- **Lead Magnet Picture or Video.** Post a picture and information about your Lead Magnet. Better yet, use an explainer video.
- **Sign Up Form.** Also on the Landing Page is your Lead Capture Form. The Lead Capture form is generated by your email service provider, (but you may add more design to it).
- **Email Auto-Responder Letters.** More on these later. which can include Product Offers & Promotions

I like the format of a video on the left side of the page, and form on the right – both above the fold. But do whatever works best for your products and your market.

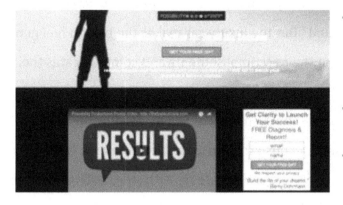

< Header
with compelling
Image & text

< Video

< Lead Capture
Form

If you have a limited budget, or if you want to get the best bang for your buck, it's a good idea to:

- Have your website built so you can manage it in house and make changes quickly.
- Learn to produce your own videos.
- Also, your website must be mobile friendly! 50% of searches are done on mobile (mostly phones), and that number is increasing. Make sure your site, form, and links work well on the phone.

(Yes, we offer these services and DIY classes, too. Notice how natural it is to build your product offers, and your Sales Funnel, by understanding your clients and their needs, along with your strengths. You are working to capture greater Lifetime Value.)

When it comes to your Lead Magnet, ask yourself:

- How can I enhance this product and make it irresistible?

- What's the "benefit behind the benefit" of this product? As an example, people don't "need" a luxury car to get around. But the luxury car makes the person feel good about their accomplishments and communicates their status to others.
Review the Psychology of Selling chapter.

- How can I push the prospects' emotional buttons with power words and phrases? With story telling? How else?

- Storytelling that people can relate to and that evokes emotions, memories, aspirations, and more.

- How do the emotional enhancers and human needs apply to your product?

See the Emotions, Needs and Power Words listed in previous chapters.

What are your Lead Magnet Opportunities?

Make your Lead Magnet
. . . "not just irresistible but also
'remarkable' as in 'worthy of remark'"

- Seth Godin

Chapter 13 - Your Compelling Front End

Let's look at the definition of the word "compel." It implies overcoming resistance by the exertion of strength, power, or duress. The strength and power we wield in the marketplace is with helping prospects relieve their pain. This is why the emotional hot buttons and power words are so important. Further, it is why we must be coming from a place of "serving" our clients – so they do not feel that we are being coercive, but instead, that we are acting in the very best interest.

I originally was going to use the word "Inspire" here, but that word is softer. We *absolutely need* the prospect to take action and buy. They need that too, or they'll be without resolution. Worse yet, if we don't compel the "Yes," they will probably end up buying from someone else with a product that won't deliver as well. And, we won't make our money!

To repeat the importance of the situation, your first "sale" is to get the person to trade their email for the value you offer. With the Lead Magnet, they give you entrée to their email inbox; you give good value in return. Now, with the Front End product you must compel action. You ask your prospect to take the next step, to, "Take out your credit card, click the 'Shopping Cart' button, and buy!"

There can be no abandoning the cart here, either. Your offer must compel the buyer to buy! Until they buy, they are not in your Sales Funnel! They remain in pain, and you miss out on income! That said, don't be pushy in the sales process. Be serving. When necessary, be firm, but always operate with their best interest in mind. There is a balancing act between encouraging them to take action and getting them more ready to do so.

Even though buying the Front End is a crucial step, remember, you probably won't make anything on these products. So, in creating your Front End, it's a good idea to use "more creativity than cash." Remember, it can take 5 to 12 "touches" before the buyer says yes. Do all you can to help them say yes, when the time and everything else is right. (Of course all this relies on the fact that they do in fact need your product. If there's not a fit, they are not a prospect. Just say "Next!"

Begin by asking, "What does your target market need?" Ask the people who subscribe to your email list, your FaceBook fans or other social media peeps, to send you their challenges or create a simple survey to find the most relevant products for your market. (You can use **Survey Monkey** for free.)

We went through this process to create your Lead Magnet. People have different expectations from a Lead Magnet. While people expect value, it doesn't need to provide a value of a $100 to $1,000. Remember Mrs. Fields and her cookies.

- Guide, report
- Cheat sheet
- Resource list
- Info-graphic
- Assessment or Test
- Interview for publication
- Coupon Discount code

- Photo or Video Opportunities
- First 20 pages of eBook
- Video training
- Free trial
- Survey
- Other

How to Make Your Offering More Compelling

There are many ways to make your offer more compelling.

Make Comparisons, Dollar Shave Club Example.
Although it is called Dollar Shave Club, they want you to spend much more than that. They lure people in with the name and then show them two pricier options that provide a lot more value than the standard one- dollar option.

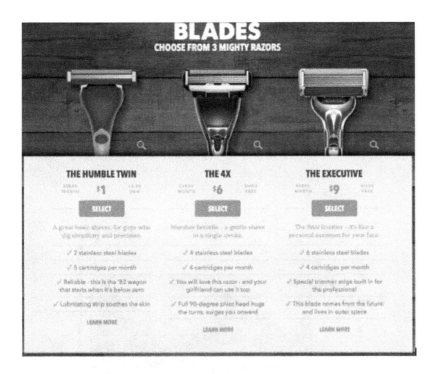

As another comparison example, Virgin Atlantic's wording for its mid-level seating is quite clever: by calling it "premium economy" rather than "business class" or something similar, it makes it seem less of a step up. But look at the huge difference in price.

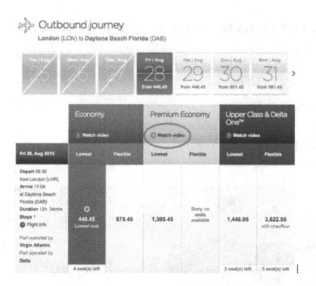

They include a short video for each of the seating options so customers can easily see all the features while they're in the process of choosing their ticket.

Mention More Products

We can learn from Amazon. When they introduced the Up Sell in 2006, using the phrase "customers who bought this item also bought this," sales increased by 35%!

Increase Perceived Value With a Bundle

If you're selling a book, you can bundle it with a Skype call or email course that works hand in hand with your book. If the bundle is both valuable and relevant, you will persuade more people to buy.

The perceived value may be that shipping costs are less if the items are purchased together. Or you can offer a discount when the two are bought together.

Value-Added – Convenience Bundle

Grocery Stores sell everything you need to make a meal. But, for example, as a convenience, at Publix Grocery Store, now you can order the ingredients for planned meals in advance and buy the package at a price that is little more than what it would cost for your to collect the ingredients yourself. The consumer gets more convenience. The grocery store ensures that the consumer buys his or her groceries at their store instead of going to buy take-out.

Use Urgency & Scarcity

Creating a sense of scarcity can increase the demand for your product and motivate people to take immediate action.

One way to scarcity in a service-oriented business is by launching a campaign that aims to find a limited number of clients. You can position this as having only a limited number of projects slots available in your business before your client base is full and you are closed to incoming work. This can be especially effective if you have a large mailing list or audience you frequently reach out to.

Selling Your Front End

Your Front End Landing Page
First, your landing page should look similar to and be compatible with and your brand, and particularly with whatever ad sent them to your landing page. Your landing page should include the same copy that you used on your ad, sales letter, or wherever it was that people saw that got the to visit your landing page.

Video
Front End Landing Page, include a sales video (1-5 minutes) and the script of the voiceover as well as a sign up form that links to the page where they give their credit card and buy.

According to Unbounce.com, "**Approximately 30% of page visitors watch your introductory video and 50% of those viewers watch the video in its entirety**". Another added benefit of adding a video is that sites that had an introductory video on their homepage saw **a 10% increase in conversion rates.**

Copy
- Your landing page should include provocative questions or statements.
- Include your list of benefits.
- Add testimonials and other social proof.

- Show your prices with its actual value (say $50) crossed out and the price you're asking (say $7). Show what percent it is they are getting off (say 85%). And, tell them why you are discounting the price so much, for example, "We want to make it a no-brainer for you to get started with us."
- In other words, give visitors everything they need in order to say yes.

What are your Front End product opportunities?

No matter who you are or what kind of
company or organization you work for
(even if that's your own business), your
number-one job is to tell your story
to the consumer wherever they are,
and preferably at the moment they are
deciding to make a purchase.

- Gary Vaynerchuk

Chapter 14 - Your Money-Making Up Sell

The Up Sell is your core product, the best part, the moneymaker of the Sales Funnel. That is why you must have a high converting Up Sell that will bring you big revenue.

The Up Sell is an immediate offer to your buyers once they've completed their purchase of your Front End offer. Of course, if they didn't buy your Front End product, odds are, they will also not buy the Up Sell. But, they might. Always remember the 12 touches to the sale. I was on a vendor's email list for a year before the right product caught my attention, at the right time, and I plunked down $1,000 on the Up Sell, although I had never bought the Front End. It happens.

The price of an Up sell is almost always higher than the Front End product because an Up Sell is an upgraded version of the Front End.

When you are writing your sales copy for your Up Sell, write it in a way where you are offering them an immediate solution or an in-depth solution that enhances the Front End product.

Remember, in the sales funnel concept, income from your Front End offer will not go to you, probably not a single cent. You'll either spend what you make from the sales funnel on promotions and advertising or give 100% commissions to affiliates that promote your Front End.

Where are you going to make your money? From the Up Sell.

Just as importantly, Up Sells increase the satisfaction of your buyers.

Serious buyers will want to buy your Up Sell s. They are actually looking forward to buying more products from you. Along their way in your Sales Funnel, they may bite on your newest Lead Magnet and then go on to buy another Front End product. That said, you make your money from the Up Sells. So, how many Up Sells should you offer? As many as your market will buy from you.
When they start the buying loop by purchasing the Front End product from you, they are already giving you the opportunity to push them further to buy something more. When they are still in the buying mood, give them something else to buy, something that will further solve their problems or make them feel good.

While the Front End product plays the role to start the loop of the buying trance, Up Sells, Down Sell, and the Backend must be there to facilitate the process. People have made the first commitment with you when they make the first purchase, so now they are going to follow your lead into the sales funnel, and into making more purchases.

Products Additions With Little or No Work

Live Q and A – You'd be surprised how much people will pay just to have access to ask you and/or your team questions on a weekly, bi-weekly or monthly basis. This 'access' level has a *very* high-perceived value. And the value is there because they get to ask you questions about their specific pains, wants, needs, desires, etc. related to the niche or market you're in. The cool thing is that you're not really creating a product. You and/or your team just have to show up!

Q and A sessions can be priceless and they really help you build rapport with your customers, while being a vehicle that is simple for you to fulfill on.

Services – Perhaps there's some kind of service you can provide (possibly outsourced) that your customers will find hugely valuable. For example, let's say your product is a course on how to take art photography. You may offer to critique your students' work, or provide special photo development and framing services. Think of what services you would like and would be willing to pay money for, and that's what you can offer to your buyers.

"When I shop, the world gets better,
and then the world is better, and
then it's not,
and I need to do it again."

- Sophie Kinsella

About The "Shopping Mood"

When you go to the store with your list, once you get into the shopping mood, you'll often end up buying things that are not on the list. The impulse purchase mindset contributes too! Shops place impulse goods where you are lining up for the cash register.

Some stores even build a "maze," lined with impulse products that you must navigate in order to get to the cash register. For example, you might not have thought of having a candy bar, but there they are, staring you down, speaking your name, so you buy. Why do stores do that? Because it works to encourage more Cross Sell purchases.

As a brick and mortar example of the importance of having more Up Sells, let's look at the local car dealer. If you buy a car for $30,000 and the dealer's cost was $28,000, then they made $2,000 in Front End profit.

But that's just the start. After the sale of a vehicle, customers are whisked away into the Business Manager's office (also known as the Finance Manager). This is where the dealer arranges financing for those who need a car loan and presents a large list of additional services.

As a smart car buyer, you should always **arrange your own financing** before visiting a dealer. But most people don't, and this is where a dealer will really pad their profits, by adding their own finance charge on top of the car loan they arrange.

Dealers can make an additional $1,000 to $2,000 in profit just on the financing alone.

In addition, they will try to sell you extended warranties, maintenance contracts, and other add-ons such as paint and fabric protection, all of which can easily add another $1,000 profit to the deal.

All in all, the back end profit could exceed Front End profit by 400% or more. This is why it's important to not only focus on the selling price of the car, but to look at the overall deal.

Here are common Up Sell suggestions from offline stores:

- A premium brand of alcohol when the customer doesn't specify one
- An extended service contract for an appliance
- Purchase a faster CPU, more RAM or a larger hard drive when servicing that customer's computer
- A pricier brand of watch that the customer hasn't previously heard of as an alternative to the one being considered
- A customer purchase a more extensive car wash package
- An upgraded spa package when the customer planned on just a massage

On the Internet, Up Sells are similar. While buyers are waiting to download the Front End product, you offer them the Up Sell. While the buyers are already buying, you offer more, while they are in the mood.

Another ways to grab customers is with comparisons, making the higher priced options look better. People want to get a bargain, to win.

Money is better than poverty,

If only for financial reasons.

- Woody Allen

Selling Your Up Sell

Provide A Picture, Even If Your Product Is Digital

Sellbrite says that the product image is the most important part of a product listing.

Potential consumers hardly buy anything without seeing it, so you need the right images to trigger a positive human behavior action.

Build Trust – Another Amazon Example
Get testimonials, ratings, and reviews.

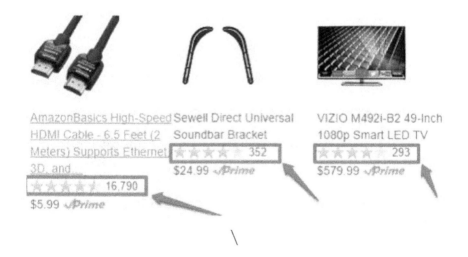

AmazonBasics High-Speed HDMI Cable - 6.5 Feet (2 Meters) Supports Ethernet, 3D, and...
★★★★★ 16,790
$5.99 √Prime

Sewell Direct Universal Soundbar Bracket
★★★★★ 352
$24.99 √Prime

VIZIO M492i-B2 49-Inch 1080p Smart LED TV
★★★★★ 293
$579.99 √Prime

Consumers believe what customers have to say way more than they believe what companies say about themselves.

Add Bonuses - Over-Deliver On Expectations.
It's the "But wait, there's more" that has been used so well in infomercials.

Over-delivering makes people happy, builds trust and creates great relationships, all of which can make people want to take action.

For retailers, free shipping is a particularly effective offer.

For an online service product, consider offering surprise gifts, add a couple free chapters of your eBook, or whatever. Always look for ways to sweeten the buyer's experience.

Offer a Guarantee
Nowadays, with buyer-friendly refund policies, buyers rarely hesitate before making a purchase, knowing that they could easily get their money back should there be discontentment in the product

- Do you have additional product you can include?

- Do you have affiliates who would like to your include their product? *Why would others do that? They get exposure; you get something free for your customers. You may get affiliate commissions, too.*

Provide a Frequently Asked Questions Page
Anticipate buyers' objections and concerns and address them upfront on a page on your website.

Here are others tips for Up Sells, and selling all your products

- Use copy that grabs attention and compels action.
- Increase conversions with video.

- Add video transcript for mobile users who don't watch the video.
- Make the Up Sell relevant to your Front End

Your Up Sell Landing Page
The Up Sell landing page is very similar to the Front End page, so refer to that section for guidelines. However, there is one important exception. If you think you might need to use a Down Sell, you'll need to prepare for that by including a few value-enhancing bonuses.

These bonuses serve two purposes.
- One, they sweeten the pot for the buyer, giving them more value.
- Two, they give you a way to make a Down Sell, by removing the bonuses so you can justify dropping the price.
- There's an additional plus if you use bonuses from vendors you "partner" with. They will offer your bonuses in their offers, promoting you. And you never can tell what might happen when you begin developing win-win relationships with other vendors.

Use Video
If your Front End is a video training program, the Up Sell can be a more comprehensive training. In fact you could have several Up Sell products that offer several programs people in your market will benefit from.
The person why buys the Front End knows that they won't be getting "the whole enchilada." To use this book as an example, there are pieces of information that there's just not room for me to include

here in the book. It's natural – and necessary – for me to offer next-step Up Sells.

For our company, Up Sells can offer more on how to create your products, how to create your video, how to write compelling copy.

These are areas I've already mentioned and that you may have already felt you will have a need for more information. What you haven't seen yet is the other subjects that I won't hardly be able to talk a lot about in this book: how to create email auto-responder letters and how to set up your Membership offer. Even more, you may have felt that you'd like to be guided through the process of actually writing, scripting, and video recording.

See why we focus on creating video programs, workbooks, and transcripts? The Up Sell offers guide people the next step – information they need or want as a fuller solution to their initial need.

See it's not about "selling" more to your customers, it's about supplying what they need, in a natural order of complexity and fuller service.

Let's look at Robbins again as an example.
On his Product page, you choose a product, check out the description, see the 30-day guarantee, and see other top selling products.

Creating Lasting Change

★★★★☆

$ 229.00

FORMAT: ☐ PHYSICAL   ☐ DIGITAL

ADD TO CART   1 ⌄

SSL Version   30-Day
Secure   Guarantee

DESCRIPTION

In times of uncertainty, people look to leaders for guidance.
Imagine having the ability to positively and profoundly affect any
individual, group or situation. What if you could influence and drive
a team to produce exceptional results and empower them to go
beyond supporting an organization to inspiring a mission-driven
movement? What if you could help a loved one or co-worker
identify what is stopping them from getting what they want in life
and give them the tools to break through?

Creating Lasting Change: The 7 Steps to Maximum Impact guides
you down the path to becoming a more effective... **READ MORE**

PRODUCT DETAILS   +

SHIPPING INFORMATION   +

BEST SELLERS
Check out some of Tony's top selling courses!

Personal Power II   Creating Lasting Change   The Time Of Y
$ 249.00 $ 229.00 - $ 249.00 $ 249.0

By including other products, people might buy more than one item,
or they might choose a different product that serves them better
now.

What are *your* Up Sell opportunities?

Applied Knowledge will never be

as expensive as ignorance is.

- Christopher Salem

Chapter 15 – Your Cross Sell Can Generate *35% More Sales

Cross Selling encourages a customer who buys your product to buy another closely related product. The difference between the Cross Sell and Up Sell is that the Up Sell is usually the next step. The Cross Sell is necessary at the same time the Up Sell is purchased. It's McDonald's saying, "Do you want fries with that?" It's Radio Shack asking if you need batteries.

Amazon is the best at the Cross Sell. With the phrase, "Frequently bought together," they get shoppers thinking of what more will help them with their current problem or desire. *Amazon attributes as much as 35 percent of it's sales to Cross Selling. **35%!**

Frequently Bought Together

Price for all three: $117.02

Add all three to Cart   Add all three to Wish List

Show availability and shipping details

☑ **This item:** Canon PowerShot ELPH 115 16MP Digital Camera (Blue) $99.50

☑ SanDisk Ultra 16GB SDHC Class 10/UHS-1 Flash Memory Card Speed Up To 30MB/s- SDSDU-016G-U46 $12.53

☑ Case Logic TBC-302 FFP Compact Camera Case (Black) $4.99 Add-on Item

Examples

1. A Life Insurance company suggests to also sign up for car or health insurance.

2. A wholesale mobile retailer suggests you choose a network or carrier after one purchases a mobile.

3. A television brand suggests you go for the home theater.

4. A laptop seller offers a mouse, pen-drive, and/or accessories.

Selling the Cross Sell

The goal of the Cross Sell is to make more money for you while creating a more satisfied customer.

You actually do your buyer a service when you offer the Cross Sell at the time they are making a purchase. Have you ever bought some kind electronic and when you get it home you find that the cord is not included, or batteries, or some other component that is really necessary? Isn't it infuriating when you think, "Why didn't they tell me I need that? Now I have to go back to the store!" That's not how to make a customer happy. So, when it comes to the Up Sell, don't think you're being pushy or "selling," you are "serving."

Notice that the process for creating your Cross Sell products is similar to that for any other of your products. To cash in on the potential for an addition 33% in sales, think of what more your customers need when they buy from you. Put yourself in their shoes. What more do they need? At the electronics store, it's batteries or a power cord that's not included. What is it for your product?

For us, the Sales funnel works hand in hand with a business website, so we offer website. Same with videos, copywriting, email auto-responders, sales letters, and more.

Notice that here is a place where you can really work with your Joint Venture partners. If you've got customers who need something that you don't offer, you can provide your partner's product. This is a win-win-win scenario. The customer needs something. Your partner does. Your partners needs another customer. You've got the customer.

What really makes these Joint Venture relationships rock is when you get paid for your referral, and your JV partner refers you, so you can make more money from their customers.

Joint Venture Opportunities, Another Reason for a Good Sales Funnel
The better filled out your Sales Funnel is, with Front End, Up Sell, Down Sell, and Back End products, the better you can be as a reciprocating partner.

What are *your* Cross Sell opportunities?

How are you cashing in on Cross Sell products?

How could you earn an extra 35%?

You control your future, your destiny.
What you think about comes about. By
recording your dreams and goals on paper,
you set in motion the process of becoming
the person you most want to be.
Put your future in good hands - your own.

- Mark Victor Hansen

Chapter 16 - Down Sell for More Sales

The down-sell is an important element in your sales funnel. Do not underestimate the power of a down-sell because when you use it the right way, it makes a huge difference to your revenue.

In previous chapters, we looked at how important it is to understand your ideal customers and their mindset. When you start to get what they are thinking, you can offer exactly what they want and value, bringing you more revenue.

The Down Sell happens in a sequence, so we'll look at that. As you already know, Up Sell offers happen right after the Front End offer. In your Up Sell offer you offer a product that enhances the Front End product.

Most importantly, offer your Up Sell with additional bonus products. In the case of off an line product, as an example, when you buy a car, they With an online offers, to give an example they may offer bonuses like free shipping, or they may actually include additional, bonus products. These add-ons make the Up Sell more attractive — if the customer is fine with the price and if they value the bonuses. But there are two things the prospect might be thinking about the Up Sell that could make them better prospects for the Down Sell.

Mindset #1: "I can't afford it."
They might think that the Up Sell is not worth the price or that they simply can't afford the product. Even though your Up Sell offer is a really great offer, some of them wouldn't take it because of the price.

Mindset #2: "I do not need the upgrades or bonuses offered."
The second possibility is that they don't think that they need the upgrades or bonuses offered in the Up Sell; so, they don't want to buy the Up Sell.

One of the reasons you can sell your Up Sell as it is priced is because of the added features or bonuses you've included. However, some of the buyers just don't see the value of the bonuses. For whatever reason, they don't want to pay the higher price.

Figuring that the Up Sell price includes the cost of the features or bonus upgrades, the prospect may think that they would buy the Up Sell alone – if that were an option. But instead of getting an upgrade bonus that is not going to be useful to them, they think they'll just pass. They'd rather live without that product than to overpay. And that's what they say, "No thanks," as they turn to walk away, or as they abandon your shopping cart.

You ask them to wait before they go. You want to offer them the Down Sell - which is the Up Well offer *without bonuses* – at a lower price. .

How the Down Sell Works

Since you know the buyers' mindset, the solution to solve the problem is by adding the Down Sell offer in your Sales Funnel. Why the down-sell works is because it understands and responds to your buyers' needs. They don't want to over pay.

When you are doing a down-sell, this is basically what you're saying to the customer:
"If you think the Up Sell is priced too high, I'll make a special offer just for you! But, for me to lower the price for you, it wouldn't be fair to those who have purchased the product paying full price. So, you will not get the bonus. And the price is lower than the Up Sell!*"*
In addition, you are creating a sense in the buyer that they are getting the same thing with a lower price in your special, promotion, down sell offer. Remember that people love a special promotion. This is why the down-sell works – it's a system that understands the buyer and is ready to serve to their needs.

Selling the Down Sell

Note that, when you are offering your Down Sell online, you remove the bonuses from the offer. As mentioned just now, to be fair to the other buyers who had bought the Up Sell offer with the bonuses and higher price, you must remove the bonuses in your Down Sell in order to drop the price.

EXAMPLE. For instance, with an online, digital product, let's say your Lead Magnet is "10 Tips that Rock Your Lead Generation." Your Front End product is "How to Get to Your Top Prospects with LinkedIn." Your Up Sell is a "Life-Changing Lead Generation Course." You could offer bonuses like "How to Use Twitter for Lead Generation" and "How to Create Your Email Auto-Responder Letters." This could be the offer from Front End to the Up Sell, with bonuses.

For your down-sell, you need to remove the bonuses that you included in the Up Sell sales copy, and then drop the price. Offer the video training course on how to do lead generation with LinkedIn, without the bonus classes.

The Down Sell operates the same with physical or offline products. We already mentioned Jessica London, but there are other examples.
Kohl's offers many price incentives with their Kohl's Cash. And most "Black Friday" offers are Down Sells, or a combination of Down Sell and Front Line products.

Now you may be wondering, "How much can I drop the price and still earn revenue from the down-sell offer?" As we've said already, know your numbers. This is a good time for you to refer back to the Client Lifetime Value (CLV) calculator.

- If the Up Sell is **$100,** can you afford to drop the price by
  $20, which then makes it **$80** for your Down Sell offer?

- If the Up Sell is **$250**, can you drop $50 and make it on **$200** for your Down Sell?

You may also want to consider authorizing your affiliates to offer a Down Sell, too. Know your numbers and you'll know whether it pencils out financially.

EXAMPLE – USE COMPARISONS

Show your prospects the highest priced item first and then the one just a little more expensive than they'd planned seems extremely cheap. This can be really effective when your customer can't afford a more expensive item. Rather than attempting to only sell them a higher-priced item, and as a result losing the sale altogether, you simply sell them a similar product that fits just above their budget.

Remember Dollar Shave Club? If people can't afford or don't see the value in the higher priced razors, point them to the lower priced product.

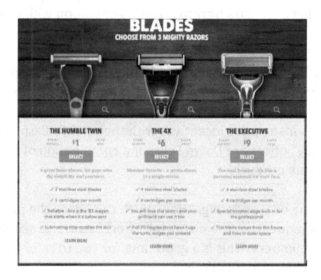

This comparison tactic is used in many kinds of product offers.

Down Selling happens a lot in traditional businesses such as auto-sales and retail. You may want a nice suit but on declining the salesperson's offer you may be shown an alternative, cheaper suit. That is a down sell (i.e. you are shown a second, lower-priced product).

Here are some useful hints and tips on Down Selling:

- Wait until you are absolutely sure they can't afford the premium product, you might sell the most expensive item after all if you keep stating it's benefits.
- Try and make it sound as though there is little difference between the two products anyway.
- If you haven't got a lower-cost version, try and sell them something else.

Note that a Down Sell is *not* the same as a discount. Whereas some element of negotiating may work in a face-to-face situation, in online marketing, offering the same product for a lower price after an initial rejection may just appears sleazy.

Every dreamer deserves to
achieve their dream.

- Berny Dohrmann

Chapter 17 - Your 2nd, 3rd & More Up Sells

The 2nd, 3rd, and your additional Up Sells provide your customers with additional benefit from the first Up Sell they bought from you. The Up Sells are also compatible with your Front End product. With this congruence, your customers always feel confident that you have the expertise to solve their problems.

The Sales Funnel can be set up a series of products that offer more and more value, and often at higher and higher prices for each Up Sell.

Or you can offer several products at different prices.

That's how what Anthony Robbins does. He's got two kinds of Front Ends.

- One - He gives low-cost (from $100 to $200), live value-packed presentations where he offers higher-priced experiences.

- Two – He has a full line of books, audio and video products that he offers on his website, with prices from $10 to $500.

When customers receive those Front End programs, they learn about Robbins' other products (which may or may not be higher priced), as well as his live programs, coaching, certification opportunities, and more.

Because Robbins is famous and he has lots of products, packaged programs, and workshop experiences, someone can enter his Sales Funnel at one of many levels. Before he became a Robbins' client, did President Clinton go to one of Robbins' workshops before he called on Robbins for his consulting services? I highly doubt it.

Further, because Robbins' helps people make changes in their thinking and behaviors, he offers training on a variety of subjects: health and wellness (including weight loss), relationships, communication, taking action, wealth, and more.

Robbins' Sales Funnel doesn't force people to buy according to his plan; and yours shouldn't either.

It might be that your customer doesn't need the Up Sell #1; but they do need the Up Sell #2 and so on.

We mentioned these businesses before.
Now let's look at them as examples of the various Sales Funnel products:

- Tim Ferris, author of "Four Hour Work Week" gives the first chapter of his book as a free Lead Magnet.

- Massage Envy gives a big discount to new customers, which is their Front End product.

- Neil Patel goes from the free Lead Magnet webinar to the Up Sell program.

- Massage Envy offers Aroma Therapy with your massage, as a Cross Sell.

- Massage Envy also offers the Membership, which is their Back End.

- Tony Robbins has high-value, expensive programs and mega-expensive one-on-one consulting as his big-ticket Back Ends.

As we've already said, the additional Up Sells should be compatible with the Front End product. Just because a customer bought your Front End and your Up Sell does not mean they will automatically buy your Up Sell #2 and beyond. They might skip that and go straight for your high-ticket Back End. Or they might become a part of your Membership program.

You should examine your customers' needs so you can predict what they need after purchasing your Front End product. In other words, you forecast a problem that the customer would encounter when using your product. Perhaps, if your product is about creating a DIY website, your Up Sell can be training them how to create compelling copy for their website.

There are always things that the customers need after they've purchased your Up Sell. To know what they are, you have to do a little bit of research.

You can apply the down-sell model in any one of your product sales funnels. After some practice using the Sales Funnel, it will become second nature to you.

You'll consider what more products your customers need after they have your Up Sell. You also need to create bonuses to be included in your Up sell. Remember, this is because you need to increase the value of your Up Sell deal and it is more important to do it in the 2nd and 3rd Up Sell where your value needs to be really high.

Let's talk how about how to reap as much profit as you can from your sales funnel, which is by including a 2nd, 3rd, and more, Up Sell s to your Sales Funnel.

Let me ask you here, knowing that we have additional products available – emails, video, copywriting, and more – do you feel that we're trying to jam more products down your throat? I hope not! The fact is, we have additional product available – and that is a service to you. Is that how you experience us?

We believe that we are the best at fulfilling your needs and our testimonials say the same thing. So, we don't want you to have to find another solution. We create the products that you will need. And it just so happens that, in doing so, our income increases.

In other words, we are "walking our talk." We teach Sales Funnels and we model with our own. It will be the same with you. You will research to determine what more your customers need and will need. And you will develop a full range of products to serve them.

What are 2nd, 3rd, and More Up Sells?

The add-on Up Sells are exactly what their name implies, more of your product to serve your customers. The 2nd Up Sell may be of greater value than the first Up Sell and the 3rd Up Sell may be a higher value than the 2nd Up Sell. As a rule, the price for each product increases according to the levels, but not always.

Let's interject here about Cross Sells. (You'll learn more about Cross Sells later.) A Cross Sell is a compatible product that works with the Up Sell. When you buy a piece of equipment at Radio Shack and they ask if you need batteries, that's a Cross Sell

The purpose of having the first Up Sell is for the customer to buy an additional or higher-priced product. Having the 2nd and 3rd is exactly the same concept but taking that method a little further.

The inclusion of 2nd and 3rd Up Sell in the Sales Funnel is an act of stretching it to get as much profit as we can.

Applying the same concept from the original Up Sell, the 2nd and 3rd Up Sells should be relevant to and compatible with all the products in the sales funnel and most importantly, the Front End product.

Without compatibility, the sales funnel would throw the customer off.

Why Do You Need a 2nd and 3rd Up Sell?

Isn't one Up Sell enough for your sales funnel? If not, how many more should you offer?

You can profit from having just one Up Sell product, of course. But, the big cost of getting leads and turning them into customers suggests that once you have a customer, you should sell them more.

Look at it this way: How much value and benefit should you provide your clients with? Isn't the answer, "As much as possible, as much as they need, as much as I can help them with?"

Besides for entrepreneurs, business is often about pushing yourself to the limit, to see how much good you can do, to see how much profit you can reap. There's no reason to settle for mediocrity.

Having a 2nd and 3rd Up Sell has already proven to be profitable. There's no reason for you to pass on an opportunity like this. No reason for you to be left out.

When to Offer Your Up Sell #2 and Beyond?

We'll talk in a bit about how you use email communications to guide your customer's path through their Sales Funnel. The importance of these communications cannot be overstated. When you keep in touch with your customer – so you know their progress with the 1st Up Sell – you'll know when to offer the 2nd Up Sell. Or you can let them know about your additional products – as a service to them – without "selling."

(You've experienced that with this book. This is all about your Sales Funnel, but there are additional pieces of information you will need to do the work yourself or you may want to get the work done for you.

For example, I've just said that the email communications are key to the success of your Sales Funnel and selling products beyond the Up Sell.)

Selling your next step Up Sell too quickly can upset a customer. They may feel annoyed that you don't realize that they don't need what you are offering yet. However, as you predict what they will need sometime in the near future, you could offer a Bundle that includes the next step product at a reduced price. That will feel like you understand them - as you offer a helpful option that is sensitive to their needs – both current and future.

In this example, the Bundle offer, while not being pushy, let's your customer know that you understand the path they are on, what they need next, and that they might like to get a bargain Bundle price. For you, that means you get the sale and the income sooner.

It's important to note that you can't do a 2nd and 3rd Up Sell willy-nilly. You need organization and proper planning. You want to help your customers feel served, you want to thrill them, and capture their loyalty – instead of having them roam off to another vendor.

Starting your own business
isn't just a job –
it's a way of life.

- Sir Richard Branson

Creating the Up Sell Script

Now, for an Up Sell to sell, it's not enough that you present sales copy on the product page only. There is an intricate method to pull off a good Up Sell offer. The offer requires good copywriting that includes a few important elements.

Establish Value
First of all, you need to establish the reason for owning the Up Sell. What do these products do? How can they help?

Let's go back briefly to what these products are because this is an important aspect. Once again, your Up Sell products are not "missing parts" of the Front End product. They are boosters or enhancements for your customers to use the first product.

So, make the reason for owning this product clear. What can these Up Sells do for them? As an example, ff your product is a do-it-yourself, do people need step-by-step guidance?

That could be the reason you can use when you're selling the product.
Communicate the difference between what they have now and how the next product provides even more value.

Establish Urgency
One technique you can always count on in making a sale is the scarcity factor. The scarcity factor is an advertising technique where the product is made available only for a limited time. For example, the offer is only available for one week and after that, the offer will expire.

It creates a sense of urgency. When the customers see that the deal is available for a short time only, and if they were to miss it then, they would miss it forever. Only then they would be more encouraged to make the purchase. The scarcity factor does magic when it comes to closing a sale.

A lot of products that you can find online utilize this method because of how effective it is. Usually, to put a little boost on the method, the sales page would incorporate a timer so that the people can see when the deal expires. With the timer running, the customer would feel compelled to make an immediate decision.

With the scarcity factor, plus the 'buying trance' that they have after making a purchase, it is easier to close a deal than ever.

Call to Action
When you're selling something online, it is more important than ever to have a call to action in your copy. The call to action completes the whole sales pitch. If you are not familiar with call to action, it is the part of a copy that convinces the customer to make a decision and to buy now.

For example, there's the "Get this product now!" or "Buy it now!" in almost every sales copy. The whole copy should be formed to point to the call to action because the call to action is the final step in securing a sale. So, it's recommended that you take your time when you want to write a call to action.

The call to action should be clear and very visible. If your call-to-action button is obscure and customers miss it, then the whole copy would fail.

Without a sense of urgency,
desire loses its value.
- Jim Rohn

Chapter 18 – Big-Bucks Back Ends

There are two types of Back End products that we'll talk about.

First are high-priced Back End products with value to match. These high-priced products are for your exclusive, elite market. Some businesses make more from their Back End than from the rest of their funnel combined. Frank Kern quit offering training products for a while and focused sharing his mega-marketing skills exclusively with clients who could afford to pay him big, big bucks. One-on-one work with high-paying clients is Kern's Back End, as of this writing, anyhow.

Next are high-earning products that can make you fortunes by the sheer volume of customers you serve. They don't have to be high-priced products because they rely on many, many people buying on a recurring, monthly basis.

We'll talk first about the High-Priced Back End.
Ask yourself, which BACK-END products have you bought?

- First Class airline tickets
- Presidential suite at hotel
- Private room at restaurant
- In-Home hair & beauty service
- VIP tickets to events

Why did you pay more for those products? Because you felt the value you received was worth the high price, right? It's the same with your products and your customers. Some people want exclusive, VIP treatment. They want more from you, so it makes sense to find ways to give them more.

The Right Back End for You
Not just any offer will do. Not all products can sell as a big-ticket Backend. Most products just don't really cut it. So, what products are good enough to be a big-ticket Backend?

Here are some Back End ideas:

1. Advanced course

2. DVD of live seminar

3. Live Seminar in Person

4. Group coaching/mastermind groups

5. Personalized coaching from you as guru

Back End workshops are often live, for a higher-perceived value. But, to create the perception of VIP, think of using high-end venues, high-quality materials, and exclusive everything.

At live events the next big-ticket workshops and events are easier to sell. There's the buyers' trance that comes over the audience, that encourages attendees to pull out their credit cards and buy more.

When it comes to the Back End, Greg S Reid says it best,

"It's expensive.

It's exclusive.

It's worth it."

- Greg S. Reid

The Big-Ticket Back End Offer

Your customers won't purchase your big-ticket Back End offer on a whim. It's expensive. Customers need to know they will get the kind of value from the Back End that you promise.

Often, only established brands can pull off the big-ticket Back End. For someone who is new in the business, selling a big ticket Back End could be an uphill battle. Imagine if you were the customer, would you willingly invest a huge sum of money on a product from someone you'd never heard of?

It depends on the customer's desire for special treatment, exclusive, prestigious, and VIP status. And it depends on your being able to deliver . . . and creating the perception that you can.

Greg S. Reid is a perfect example of what it takes to offer a Back End that rocks.

- For his book, Reid interviewed **celebrities** and business people. By association, this improved his own celebrity.

- His book, "Three Feet From Gold," was published **in cooperation with Napoleon Hill Foundation,** known for the classic, "Think and Grow Rich," which lends credibility.

- He's a popular **Keynote Speaker**

- He has **Business Celebrity Associates:** Berny Dohrmann, David Corbin, John Assaraf, Sharon Lechter

- He is a vision-into-action kinda guy and is **producing the movie,** "Wish Man," with Frank Shankwitz, founder of Make a Wish

- Secret Knock is one of his Back End programs. With business celebrities like Bob Proctor, Les Brown, Mark Victor Hanson regularly speaking and/or attending, "it's expensive, it's exclusive, it's worth it."

Reid has done what it takes to attract and sell his big-ticket Back End. Everything about Reid speaks of his brand, "cool and prosperous."

The Back End is usually offered after a customer has already bought from you, knows the quality of your work, and trusts that you will deliver big-value results for the big price they pay.

There are no hard and fast rules with the Sales Funnel. For example, a person can hear about Reid's "Secret Knock" event, take out their credit card, book their room and flight, and go. But, not everyone qualifies as an attendee.

But, for people to learn about your Back End and to be convinced to do that means that you have done what it takes, like Greg S. Reid does.

The choice is yours:

up your action

or reduce your goals & dreams

- Eric Lofholm

Big-Ticket Back End Idea Details

The Big-Ticket product has to be of a very high value for the customers, and able to generate huge profit for you.

Here are some ideas of products you can sell as a big-ticket product.

Live One-to-One Coaching

Coaching is where you offer guidance to your customer, or client, in your field of expertise. If your expertise is how to start a business, then you have to guide clients and give them pointers through the whole process of opening a business.

Requirements for a Coach
Coaching is a very profitable and rewarding but you need to actually be an expert in something before you can teach. The saying, "Those who can't do, teach," does not apply in the coaching world. People want to see proof that **you've been successful** before you can establish yourself as a coach.

As a coach, you also need to be a **confident speaker**. How would you be a coach if you were not an outgoing person that is full of energy and enthusiasm?

Coaching requires interaction. Though communication is easier with the Internet, you need live interaction in a coaching program.

Therefore, even though you can **communicate via Skype or Google** Hangout, you need to find the right time to do so.

If you offer your **services internationally**, your clients and customers will be from different parts of the world. They might even be directly from the other side of the world from where you are. This isn't a problem with packed programs. But if you are coaching, that means you'll have to work around time zones.

The price range for a one-on-one coaching program is generally from **$500** to **$25,000** or more.

Live Group Coaching

In a group coaching engagement, you are interacting with more than one individual at a time. Just like coaching, you would need expertise in a field before you can go on promoting your group-coaching program. It's easier to get clients and customers if you were already an established name in your industry.

The price range for group coaching, however, is lower than individual coaching as it's a shared service. The price range of group coaching is from **$200** to **$5,000 or more**.

Certification and Licensing Programs

Coaching program and group coaching programs require commitment and take a lot of your time. There is another way that you can make big profits with an "evergreen" product that you create once and continue to profit from.

A certification program is where you train and "certify" others and give them the rights to use and sell your content. Licensing is where you sell rights to your program. So, you create the content and you extend your market and reach by having others use your content, either in a certification arrangement or as licensees.

There's more for you to learn about these. Certifications and/or licensing are great ways for you to profit. If you think it's a fit for your product, look into them more. They are legal agreements, so you'll need to get guidance and contracts from a business attorney.

Selling The Back End

The Back End must deliver it's own unique set of value and benefits. Your reputation and "celebrity" in your industry will make a difference too. The list of others you have attracted to your Back End offer will matter. When Back End prospects see that others have bought, they'll say, "So and so Big Shot jumped in, I guess I will too."

- Getting publicity, especially in respected publications, can help.

- To be a published author and speaker, as well as having impressive connections can make a difference.

- Doing presentations at prestigious conferences gets you in front of the right people.

- Retargeting ads, where people have visited your site, then are presented ads from Facebook or Google because of the "cookies" on their history work well. (Cookies are how the Internet knows where you've visited.) In the case of ads, it directs ads to be shown to those who already showed interest in you by visiting your site.

- Joint Ventures. Working in cooperation with other providers who offer complimentary products really work well here.

For your Big-Ticket Back End you need a few customers paying you fees for exclusive products, services, events or more. Now don't think a "few" means a dozen. A few can be hundreds of people who show up for an exclusive event, each happily shelling out $5,000 for a two-day event.

The thing about the Back End is, You Can Sell Less Product and Make More Money!

An example will help. Let's say you sell an E-Book for $17. How many E-Books do you have to sell to make $5000?

The answer is 295! That's a lot of E-Books!

Let's say instead, you sold an information product that consisted of 6 CDs and instruction manual. And it sells for $297. How many copies do you have to sell to make $5000?

17 copies!

Or, to take this a bit further, say you had a complete home study system which included 20 CDs, 20 DVDs, 3 training manuals and 1 Year of Free Access to a **Membership** Site. How much would that be worth? How about $1,499? How many of these systems do you have to sell to make $5,000?

ONLY 4 copies!

The point is that, with higher prices, you can sell much less product and make more money! That means you don't need as many leads, and lead generation is costly so that's important. Isn't it a good idea to invest in creating more products, and a solid **Back End**?

The creation and production costs of a similar big ticket information product, although high, are still pretty low really, just the cost of CDs, DVDs, and their cases, binders, burning the CDs or DVDS and printing out your hard copy information. Maybe $50, and that might be on the high side. Figure in warehousing, fulfillment, shipping, and customer service, and say that's another $50.

On a $1500 product, your net profit is still $1,400!!!

And many offer physical products because they are perceived to be of even higher value than digital products. They found that their response rates were higher when selling a physical product, as compared to the digital equivalent.

Further, product returns are actually less with Big Ticket items because the customers themselves are more invested in the product.

To have a successful Back End that optimizes the ROI of the investment you've made in lead generation, your lead magnet, and your Front End – you need a Back End that performs in one of two ways, or both.

Ticket To Multi-Millions
Dan Kennedy said he became a millionaire by selling to many, many people. But he became a multi-millionaire selling to a much smaller, select group of his existing customers. The bigger spenders were Kennedy's big-ticket sub list!

Treat the people on this sub list as if they are very special. They are. You should be sending them some of your most valuable information along with unexpected bonuses, for free!

Winners Do What Others Aren't Willing To Do
Face it, You're going to do one or more of the following activities:
write a one page sales letter, create a direct mail campaign, develop
product, build JV relationships, create a website landing page, drive
traffic to the site, and basically do all the other things we do as
marketers, and more. And that's going to be necessary for every
product you sell!.

Wouldn't you rather sell a higher value, higher priced, huge profit
margin, big-ticket item than a $20 eBook? Now, don't get me
wrong, you need to have your book, for all the reasons we
described earlier.

And, hey, it can happen that your books sell millions of copies. Co-
authors of the" Chicken Soup for the Soul" series of books, Jack
Canfield and Mark Victor Hansen know that books *can* turn into
bucks. But that's not usual.

Selling Your High-Ticket Back End

To sell High-Ticket products, you must present yourself as a high-
ticket provider. Period. We already gave Greg S. Reid as an
example of a high-end provider.

Here is a situation where the saying fits, "You've gotta spend money
to make money."

Your events should be at five star venues. Your website and
collateral materials should be first class. Your social media should
show your luxury life, so people feel that you are worth following –
and buying – as a high-end personality. Let people see you hanging
out with celebrities. Look like you are "in" with the crowd of those
living a luxury lifestyle.

The product you're offering as a Back End is especially for your VIP customers. Now, it's not something that is entirely new for them, but to them, it feels exclusive, VIP, not for everyone. The high-ticket market wants that; give them what they want.

Your 2ⁿᵈ Back End for Big Money

To speak to every business owners' dreams of big bucks, I have two words to say about a Back End they can implement: MEMBER and SHIP. Add a membership to your Back End and your ship is about to come in.

Membership, the word reminds us of the old American Express slogan, "Membership has its privileges." Indeed. For your members and for your Sales Funnel.
For business, Membership is all about Automatic Recurring Billing (ARB). What more can a company that sells anything wish for than automatic recurring billing? Yipee!

Anyone who joins a club knows they are going to pay a monthly fee. The key word here is "join." Whenever you can convince a customer to join your organization, the concept of an automatic recurring bill is virtually assured.

Let's look at some Membership examples:

Netflix versus RedBox
These are both popular business models. But the proof of the better model is in the earnings. Earnings were $1.89 billion in 2014 for Redbox versus $5.50 billion for Netflix. Netflix has delivered on it's exclusive club idea, creating content that can only be found on Netflix, like "House of Cards," "Orange is the New Black", among others.

For Netflix, payments are for sure and automatic. For RedBox, payments depend on shoppers making a conscious decision to rent a movie at the time of payment.

Amazon Prime
Amazon keeps adding to the exclusive benefits they give their members. Free two-day shipping, unlimited streaming movies and TV shows, download free music, and ability to borrow books – all for $99 a year or $10.99 a month.

Who can possibly resist?
How can you learn from Amazon?

Dollar Shave Club
We mentioned them before as an example of comparison as a way to encourage higher-priced purchases. With the Shave Club, we have a perfect example that any product can be turned into a "club." Razor blades, seriously?

Many Kinds of Memberships
Wine clubs, massage club, car sash club, florist club, preferred pricing at hotels; there are many kinds of ARBs.

Why do Memberships Work?

- We don't want to be left out

- We want preferred pricing

- We want VIP treatment

- We want to be special

So, how can your business offer a Membership?

Try this: decide that you want to offer a Membership to your customers (and prospects) then work backward.

Creating the idea for your Membership is a great subject for brainstorming.

Survey and do research to discover what your people want. Keep your eyes and ears open. Berny Dohrmann, founder of CEO Space International started his Platinum Level Membership when one of his members asked for it. Now he keeps listening for what more his members want. CEO Space's Platinum Membership is not a monthly ARB program. But, it does provide his high-end people with big-ticket value.

If you have a monthly ARB Membership, members will expect something of value from you every month. Odds are you'll need to perform and maybe upload new content every month to satisfy – and thrill - your members.

As a courtesy, send your members reminder emails to sell them on the value of their membership, and to ensure that they receive and benefit from the Membership perks they are paying for.
For your Membership Back End, you need a gazillion customers paying you Automatic Recurring Billings every month. Don't you just love the sound of that? Automatic Recurring Billings! Build a valuable Membership offer and you can count on significant income, automatic billing every month!

Selling Your Membership Back End

Lets talk about selling your Membership Back End. You can treat this like another Up Sell offer. In fact, some people may prefer to call it an Up Sell. As we said before, don't get hung up on names of the products; let's focus on making money. The reason we call it a Back End is because it can be such a huge source of recurring income.

Refer to the earlier section on "Selling Your Up Sell." As with all your products, you'll need a landing page, video, sales script, social proof, email sign-up form and auto-responder letters. You may want to provide other special items as well. There are many promotional items available: shirts, mugs, computer bags, and more. You may want to make these available for free to your members.

Of course, you'll also need the technology platform for your Membership. We like to build our sites and landing pages with WordPress, and there are membership plugins available.

Your Back End Sales Page Should Include:

- Compelling Text

- Video

- Testimonials

- Social Proof

- Call to Action

Also, Include what those benefits *mean* to your prospects. It's all about selling and buying:

- Compelling Text – that hits their emotional buttons . . . and sells

- Video – grabs attention and builds interest in buying

- Testimonials – so people feel confident in buying

- Social Proof – so they see you as capable and trustworthy

- Call to Action – so they go to your product page & buy

As you can see, it is far easier to read, and also to write, this lists than to just talk about your product in one long, cluttered paragraph.

You can use sentences and paragraphs, but lists are easier to read online.

When to Sell Your Membership Back End?

The best time to make a Membership Back End offer is immediately after the initial sale is made. That's when your customer's desire to buy again is at its greatest. Often times the "Thank You" page for most websites is overlooked as a profit center. Big mistake.

Your "Thank You" page should reassure the customer that the order has been processed and then it should make them another offer that compliments the purchase that the customer just made.

For example: lets say you have a site where you sell a $97 with workbook and video. On the "thank you" page, you would confirm their order and offer the buyer the opportunity to "Click Here" to watch a free four-minute video on how to automate their client referral process with the use of another one of your products – an email auto-responder program. The four-minute video leads them into a 21-day series – a Back End product.

Back End: The First 21 Days

Consider the first 21 days after a purchase is made as your window of opportunity. The sooner you communicate your Back End offer with your Up Sell customer in that time, the better results you can expect. Any product or service that can benefit the customer's purchase should be systematically offered and reinforced.

It goes without saying that this works best when your initial Front End product is quality, has depth and offers a high ROI for the buyer.

As an example, "Want to know more of my money multiplying secrets and clever tactics for creating more free time in your schedule while adding more income streams? Be sure to check out my **Mentors Membership Program** (its not for everyone... but maybe it's for you.)

Set a goal to achieve something that is so big,

so exhilirating, that it excitess you

and scares you at the same time.

- Bob Proctor

Chapter 19 - Follow-Up Emails that Sell

It's true, "The fortune is in the follow up."

And email remains the most efficient, cost effective method for following up with prospects and customers. Of course you also use phone calls and other methods, but email is the best.

An important part of the Sales Funnel Blueprint is the emails that you use to follow up.

A good entrepreneur knows that selling doesn't stop after a transaction is made. Not even after all the Up Sells, ARP, & Back End. Remember the 12 Touches to the Sale? That can be for each product you sell. Emails work.

What Are Follow-Up Emails?

Follow-up emails are emails sent to the subscriber after they first sign up, and to the buyer after each purchase is made, and at many other steps along the way.

Usually, after a purchase is made, the buyer receives a "Thank You" email. This expression of gratitude is a good way to start a quality relationship between you and your customer. However, that's not the only reason for sending follow-up emails.

In the "Thank You" email, you also include contact details or help desk should any problem arises from using the product. This includes all your contact details, of course.

So, how many emails should you send? As many as it takes to fully serve your customer and to fully optimize your ROI.

However, you shouldn't be sending emails all at once! Each of them should be sent according to a strategy, probably at a few days' intervals.

There is a rhythm in marketing that you should follow in order for your products to sell. You do not want to annoy the customers by sending them to many emails. (This is a topic for you to test, to determine which is the best degree of frequency and time of day for you to send.)

Use an Attention-Grabbing Subject Line

It's the first thing that readers will see. The subject line will decide whether or not they will open your email. However, grabbing attention is not the only challenge. You also have to write a subject line that is less than 50 characters!

The reason for this is because beyond the 50th character in an email subject line will be replaced with an ellipsis. Therefore, they can't really see the full subject line, leaving your subject line incomplete and untidy.

To write an attention-grabbing subject line, it wouldn't work if you were to write the whole subject line in a small case lettering. Experiment and test to determine what works best for your customers.

Here are 20 Email Subject Lines That Work:

1. Reason Why. This subject line shares "why" they should do something

2. Benefit. "Lose Weight While You Sleep."

3. Question. "Do You Think You Can Still Get Rich?"

4. Testimonial. Matthew McConahey Can Afford any car; He Drives a Lincoln
5. How To. How to Make $50k a Month
6. News. 10 IPOs that Cold Double in 12 Months
7. Fascination. Discover the 10 Secrets of Successful Entrepreneurs
8. Target. For Startups, Here's What You Need Next
9. Personalized. "Your annual goal," "Quick question," "I hope all is well"
10. List. Best Tips for Start Ups
11. Intriguing Promises. "One more thing," Want a Four Hour Work Week?
12. Teaser. I Was Scared . . . y Biggest Client Almost Quit!
13. Seasonal. HOLIDAY Offer
14. Keywords. E.g., Small Business Success Depends on You
15. Command. E.g. Stop Leaving Money on the Table
16. Urgency. "Last Chance for This Offer"
17. Connect. "Sales Funnel Training for YOUR COMPANY"
18. Referral. "NAME referred me to you"
19. Human. "You are not alone," "Good morning, NAME"
20. Direct. "Who's in charge of reaching sales goals at COMPANY"

Copywriting

QuickSprout says, "Copywriting is the art and science of writing copy (words used on web pages, ads, promotional materials, etc.) that sells your product or service and convinces prospective customers to take action. In many ways, it's like hiring one salesman to reach all of your customers."

When it comes to copywriting, there's not room to say much in this book, and it's an important subject. As we've said many times, know your market, and work to understand their needs and motivations.
Review the Psychology of Selling Chapter, including Power Words.

Always remember, people buy emotionally and justify with logic.

Each person is different, with different emotional needs and personality traits.

This is how TV Shopping networks sell features, benefits, and the "What's in it for Me."
"This car is super stylish and with great gas mileage, which means you turn heads while helping the environment."

There's often more than one way to make things work. Pay attention to what works best for your market and products.

Copywriting can be one of the scariest and most productive elements of your Sales Funnel. Don't expect to be an ace copywriter immediately. Relax. That you are connecting and staying in touch with your prospects and customers at all puts you way ahead of the pack.

Remember, email is still the most efficient method for staying in touch with your list.

There are Several Types of Follow-Up Emails:

- 1st Email: Thank You

- 2nd Email: Tips

- 3rd Email: Hidden Tips

- 4th Email: Unannounced Bonus

- 5th Email and On: Promotional

1st Email: Thank You

The first email you should send to the buyers is the 'Thank You' email.

You express gratitude to the customers for purchasing your product; a token of appreciation. But it should also contain your contact details and refund policy for the product.

Example:
> Dear [customer],
> Thank you for purchasing [product name]! We hope you enjoy this product and we wish you all the best in using it. If you have any problems with it, and we doubt that you will, you can contact us at [vendor email]. We have a 30-day refund policy should you feel dissatisfied with our product. Good luck and thank you!
> [vendor]

In your email, ask if they might need one of your Cross Sell products, if so, by all means, offer that here.   And mention your next product.

The Thank You email is the most often neglected selling opportunity. **Remember, the best time for people to buy is when they just bought something. Your time is now!**

You can even give them a receipt here, as well. It's best to have the receipt attached to the email instead of it being part of the email.

Let them know you'll be sending them another email right away with details for using the product they bought.

2nd Email: Tips

For the 2nd email that you send to them, it's all about using the product. Just give them a little bit of pointers on how to best use your product to the fullest. You'll check in on them to see how they're doing with the product.

Example:

> Hey [customer],
>
> How's the [product] coming along? Here are some tips for you:
> * [tip #1]
> * [tip #2]
> * [tip #3]
>
> We hope you get the best out of this product.
>
> If you have any problems or enquiries, don't hesitate to contact us at [vendor email].
>
> Best wishes,
> [vendor]

Of course, as the vendor, you'd want your customers to be happy with your product and services. Sharing tips here is a great way to do that.

Plus, you want to encourage them to actually use the product. You don't want them to return it. And they can't be fully satisfied – and understand how well you deliver for them unless they use your product.

Your customers will appreciate the gesture, thus, strengthening your buyer-vendor relationship. This will pave the way for you to be a trusted and respected provider.

3rd Email: Hidden Tips

Just like the previous email, share some more tips here.

For example:

> Hey [customer],
>
> How's it going? Here are some more tips for you to use [product].
>
> * [tip #4]
> * [tip #5]
> * [tip #6]
>
> We hope you get the best out of this product.
>
> Should you have any enquiries or problems, please do send us an email at [vendor email].
>
> Thank you,
> [vendor]

Here in this email, just share some tips that you might have left out in the previous email. Sell these tips as 'hidden tips' so that the customers would feel appreciated.

4th Email: Unannounced Bonus

The fourth email is where you offer them the unannounced bonus, which is the big-ticket Backend offer.

Having a big-ticket Backend offer is a great way to maximize the sales funnel. It is the most valuable product in the sales funnel and it also can generate the most profit.

It is tempting to sell this big-ticket Backend offer immediately after the sales funnel. However, because this product is so valuable and pricey, you need to offer them a few days after the actual purchase. The best wait is 3-7 days after the purchase.

Example:

Hello [customer],

Great news! I have this bonus to offer you that is exclusive to buyers who are truly serious about [*product*].

Introducing the [*Backend product*].

Now, this is only offered to people who are really serious, though. I do not offer it to anyone else. With this product, you can:

* [*feature #1*]
* [*feature #2*]
* [*feature #3*]

Get this product here: [*product page link*]

Best wishes,
[*vendor*]

To sell a big-ticket Back End offer requires patience on your part. You have to gain the buyers' trust. The most important way you do this by making them happy with your product first.

The previous two emails sent are for this purpose exactly, so that they're happy with the product you've sold to them and they grow to trust you as a vendor.

Not following up with your prospects

is the same as filing up your bathtub

without first putting

the stopper in the drain.

- Michelle Moore

5th Email Onwards: Promotional Emails

The fourth email was the last of that sales funnel. The fifth email and onwards are promotional emails for other products that you might have.

By now, you should know the importance of capturing emails from leads - and from your customers - so you can follow up, build the relationship, sell more of your products.

Auto-Responder Emails
Email follow up is one of the essential keys to you Sales Funnel success. After you have put yourself in your prospects' and customers' shoes, you compose letters to move them forward in the funnel. Each step along the way, the letters are designed to respond to where they are now, to show you understand and care, and, to move them toward a "Yes."

View the "12 Touches" infographic we presented earlier to remember that from initial contact, to Lead Magnet, to Front End product, to Up Sell product purchases, Cross Sell, as well as your Back End – email communications drive the process in the most efficient and effective way.

That's not to say that phone calls, online ads, and greeting cards don't have a place in the Sales Funnel – they certainly do.

Greeting Card Follow-Up

Sometimes, you meet someone who's a great prospect but you can't reach them. It's very frustrating to get stuck in phone tag. And emails can be overlooked and unopened.

The fact is, in today's online world, the high-touch of an actual card sent through the mail can be very effective for following up and connecting.

You can learn more about greeting card follow up at **www.Jerrymailhot.com** or call him at 858-444-6005.

Full disclosure, I partner with Jerry with the Greeting Card Follow Up System. I'm involved in that business because I believe in getting the best ROI from leads, and I believe in the greeting-card method. It keeps people – and opportunities – from falling through the cracks.

Chapter 20 - 85 Ways To Thrill With Your Customer Experience

Customer experience includes all the events experienced by customers before and after a purchase are part of the customer experience.

I'll begin this piece by setting the stage for the 85 points about the customer experience with a quote:

> *"Find out what your customers want and give them that."*
> - Anonymous

Wharton's professor of marketing, Barbara E. Kahn suggests there are three phases:

1. The customer experience includes stimulation to all sensory, emotional, rational and physical aspects, which can help to create a memorable experience for the consumer.
2. Product: Companies manufacture goods or services and offer them the best way possible.
3. Market orientation: Some consideration of customer needs and segmentation arises, developing different **marketing mix** bundles for each one.
4. Customer experience: Adding to the other two factors some recognition of the importance of providing an emotionally positive experience to customers.
5. Listen attentively so you understand what customers need and want.
6. Intend to make your customers happy and take steps to do so.

7. Your customers are your "diamonds;" treat them as valuable.
8. You get all your money from other people; treat them with respect and consideration.
9. For good customer care, train our people with systems that ensure that customers are not just "satisfied," but "thrilled."
10. Take responsibility for your customer's experience.

   *"Although 80% of **businesses** state that they offer a "great customer experience, this contrasts with the 8% of customers expressing satisfaction with their experience."* - James Allen

11. Consider Disney (The happiest place on earth) and Ritz Carlton (Ladies and gentlemen serving ladies and gentlemen) as your role models.
12. Set your company's standard for interacting with customers: listen for understanding, never raise your voice, and smile.
13. Be consistent with customer interaction – always do #12 above, with no excuses.

14. If you make a misstep with a customer, don't just apologize, make it up to them. (But do apologize)
15. Brainstorm ways to get new ideas for increasing the customer experience.
16. Survey customers to discover their needs and wants.

17. Look to other industries to get ideas about how to thrill your customers.
18. Develop a swipe file of methods other companies (not in your industry) use to thrill their customers.
19. Make plans for upgrading your customer's experience, and implement them.
20. Use what you know about your customer's needs to assess the solutions you provide. Do your products and services "satisfy" or "thrill"?
21. Discover how to measure your customer's experience.

22. Define your customer's needs. To take misunderstanding and misunderstanding out of the equation work to be clear, concise, and accurate in your description.
23. Establish criteria for the needs discovery process.
24. Dig deeper to find your "diamonds." What additional needs are not yet met?
25. Find ways to fulfill more of your customer's unmet needs.
26. When you understand needs, you can be more on target. For example, you can create products that deliver what your people want.

27. Communicate customer needs with everyone in your organizations, so everyone is working to create "customer thrills."
28. Ask yourself: what "thrills" your customers? Your prospects? Your market?
    For example, Bill Walsh, of Power Team International, hosts parties for his customers, in penthouse suites, with business celebrities in attendance.
29. Ask yourself: how can *you* create thrilling experiences for your customers?
    What if you don't have a big budget? (I am doing a show, "Joy & Success" with a 10-minute format that gives small business guests exposure (FREE), while providing helpful "edutainment" for the audience.)
30. Invest in your customer service. Don't leave customers frustrated or unhappy. How do you care for customers?

Catherine Courage at Google suggests:

Google

31. Develop a five-year plan for increasing the customer experience.
32. Use storytelling to truly connect with customers.
33. "Don't think, 'I sent an email and posted on social media,' therefore you communicated. No, you just sent something out." To communicate better, you often need to understand storytelling and what will resonate with people.
34. Consider using storytelling in your communications – in email campaigns, presentations, and with other customer interactions.
35. Learn more about the storytelling process.
36. Use the story arc to add impact, and entertainment value, to your ongoing communications. Don't just inform – educate and entertain.

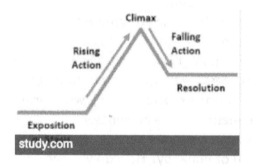

37. Use ideas for effective leadership in your customer interactions. Read (or re-read) leadership books and apply the organizational principals in your customer care.
38. Find role models for great client experiences – and learn from them.
39. Ask: What affects customer satisfaction?
40. Ask: How quickly can you get people on board?
41. Ask: How does customer experience impact revenue?

42. Ask: How does customer experience impact customer retention?
43. Understand that how you interact with customers makes a difference.
    Positive experiences equal loyalty, referrals, and bottom line improvement.
44. Help others on your team buy-in to the customer experience philosophy.

From Adobe:

45. "Connect with customers as if your future depends on it. It does."
46. "Reach for the ah-ha moment."
47. Provide a great mobile experience.
48. People use devices 50% of the time. Be responsive.
49. In all your communications, be compelling. Personal.
50. Look for ways to wow customers.
51. For deeper relationships, deliver deeper experiences.
52. Be so engaging and on time that you leave your customers wondering how you did it.
53. Be your best self. All day. Every day.
54. Create the right digital foundation.
55. Provide impressive content.
56. Develop relevant customer experiences.
57. Learn the "New Normal: Customer Experience First."
    https://adobe.ly/2vkgiYC
58. Customers are more engaged. Giving them what they need is both possible . . . and required.
59. Your people, processes, and products must respond to customer wants.
60. Model after disrupters:
61. Analyze the customer experience.
62. Define the problems and develop small, solvable pieces.

63. Brainstorm ideas and set realistic plans.
64. Prototype – quickly.
65. Test
66. Evaluate - keep customer experience at the forefront.
67. Implement quickly and be prepared to pivot quickly.
68. Understand your customer's delight – or lack of it – and adjust.
69. Assess your digital (and off line) capabilities.
70. Improve your capabilities as needed to create the wow.
71. Rinse and repeat. Your new innovation quickly becomes your customer's minimum expectation.
72. Certain types of experiences may involve different aspects of the individual person such as emotional, physical, intellectual or even spiritual.
73. Automation tools help organize customer information better. Use them.
74. Make your products and message stand out. Consumers are able to easily compare two similar products or services together.

75. Provide a great customer experience and gain a competitive advantage.
76. Understand the customer and experiment with what provides most positive results.
77. Engagement with customers is part of the process.
78. Create an experience: peace of mind, relaxation, excitement, special treatment
79. Create a feeling: your customer is special, unique, heard, and responded to.
80. Although 80% of businesses state that they offer a "great customer experience," according to author James Allen, this contrasts with the 8% of customers expressing satisfaction with their experience.

From author, James Allen

81. Design: A positive perception of the customer experience relies upon, designing the correct incentive for the correctly identified consumer, offered in an enticing environment.

82. delivery: a company's ability to focus the entire team across various functions to deliver the proposed experience.

83. development ultimately determines a company's success, with an emphasis on developing consistency in execution.

84. Implement "voice of customer" research. Monitor through surveys, targeted studies, or observational studies

85. "Conversion (of customers to loyal customers) is 100 percent dependent on an elegant remarketing to that client. So I would say it is one of our most pivotal marketing levers."
Johanna Tzu, CMO, James Allen

Customers happily pay more for a
great customer experience.

- Tony Bodoh

Chapter 21 - What is Next?

As we've talked about in this book, there are many steps involved in creating, and implementing your Sales Funnel. It's not easy, but it is simple. And if it seems hard at times, oh well. If it were easy, everyone would be doing it, and your opportunities would not be so great. Success is often overlooked because it shows up wearing overalls and looking like work.

With those steps you've learned, what's next is implementing. Like any mountain, the project can seem daunting. Make it easier on yourself, take a one-step-at-a-time approach. The order of step taking is laid out in the Infographic of the Sales Funnel.

This book gives you an overview of the process. We have created one-step-at-a-time Workbooks, where we essentially take you by the hand and provide the actions, tools, and methods that will guide your progress.

Or, you may want to consider our Done For You services. From parts of the Sales Funnel, to the whole shebang, we have a team of twenty experts standing by, waiting to serve you.

Customers don't expect you to be perfect.
They do expect you to
fix things when they go wrong.
- Donald Porte

Our Mission

It's out aim to empower small business success in America. Seriously. The Sales Funnel training and services are part of the over all project to reach that goal.

Check out our websites:

http://BarbaraLoraine.com About our biz services

http://SmallBizSuccessAmerica.com About our events

http://TheElephantInYourRoom.info About our movie

http://JoyRadioNetwork.com About our interview show

LETTER FROM THE AUTHOR

I believe that small business is *the* key to growing the American economy, while providing the freedom and fulfillment that leads to better living for each family and community. I believe in your, in your possibilities for money-making and difference-making.

While traveling the country to make the movie, The Elephant In Your Room, I interviewed people with all kinds of small business success stories. These fearless entrepreneurs were of all ages, all ethnicities, and different kinds of circumstances. They had much in common. They all followed a formula that works.

Using a Sales Funnel is an important key to success.

Getting customers is the hard – and expensive – part. By learning more about our customers, by creating more products, by truly serving their needs, we serve our customers better, build more income, and create more jobs. And that's what we all want, isn't it?

You can do it! I can't wait to hear your success story!

Best Wishes,

Barbara Loraine,
Possibility Productions Group, LLC

www.ingramcontent.com/pod-product-compliance
Lightning Source LLC
Chambersburg PA
CBHW071152050326
40689CB00011B/2080